UNDERSTANDING

ALBERT
CAMUS

by DAVID R. ELLISON

UNIVERSITY OF SOUTH CAROLINA PRESS

Library of Congress Cataloging-in-Publication Data

Ellison, David R.
    Understanding Albert Camus / by David R. Ellison. — 1st ed.
        p. cm. — (Understanding modern European and Latin Ameri-
can literature)
    Includes bibliographical references (p.) and index.
    ISBN 0-87249-705-4
    1. Camus, Albert, 1913–1960—Criticism and interpretation.
I. Title. II. Series.
PQ2605.A3734Z6388   1990
848'.91409—dc20

90-37452

CONTENTS

EDITOR'S PREFACE

Understanding Modern European and Latin American Literature has been planned as a series of guides for undergraduate and graduate students and nonacademic readers. Like its companion series, *Understanding Contemporary American Literature,* the aim of the books is to provide an introduction to the life and writings of prominent modern authors and to explicate their most important works.

Modern literature makes special demands, and this is particularly true of foreign literature, in which the reader must contend not only with unfamiliar, often arcane artistic conventions and philosophical concepts, but also with the handicap of reading the literature in translation. It is a truism that the nuances of one language can be rendered in another only imperfectly (and this problem is especially acute in fiction), but the fact that the works of European and Latin American writers are situated in a historical and cultural setting quite different from our own can be as great a hindrance to the understanding of these works as the linguistic barrier. For this reason, the UMELL series emphasizes the sociological and historical background of the writers treated. The peculiar philosophical and cultural traditions of a given culture may be particularly important for an understanding of certain authors, and these will be taken up in the introductory chapter and also in the discussion of those works to which this information is relevant. Beyond this, the books will treat the specifically literary aspects of the author under discussion and will attempt to explain the complexities of contemporary literature lucidly. The books are conceived as introductions to the authors covered, not as comprehensive analyses. They do not provide detailed summaries of plot since they are meant to be used in conjunction with the books they treat, not as a substitute for the study of the original works. It is our hope that the UMELL series will help to increase knowledge and understanding of the European and Latin American cultures and will serve to make the literature of those cultures more accessible.

Professor Ellison's *Understanding Albert Camus* fills the need for an up-to-date, comprehensive study in English. It stresses the political and cultural context and does not attempt to separate Camus's *oeuvre* artificially into "philosophical" works, on the one hand, and "literary" on the other. Rather, Ellison reveals fundamental thematic continuities linking all the major works. Camus is shown not only to be an original inventor of literary forms, but also a moralist and modern humanist.

J.H.

ACKNOWLEDGMENTS

The purpose of the following pages is to elucidate the principal literary works of Albert Camus by examining them both in their formal specificity and in their historical-cultural context. Although the readings offered in this book are those of the author and his responsibility alone, I would like to acknowledge two important debts: first, to Herbert R. Lottman, author of *Albert Camus: A Biography,* on whose acute observations I have relied throughout when examining Camus's life, notably the role of the "Algerian crisis" in it; and to the students of French 355 (Mount Holyoke College, Spring 1988), whose commitment to the close reading of Camus's fictional works made this study both possible and enjoyable. Thanks, therefore, to Clare Doyle, Suzanne Flynn, Leila Amin-Arsala, and Laura Del Savio.

ABBREVIATIONS

Book titles cited in the text have been abbreviated as shown below. Page numbers refer to the edition cited in parentheses following each title.

C = "Conférence du 14 décembre 1957" (In *Essais,* Pléiade, 1965)

CA = *Caligula,* suivi de *Le Malentendu* (Folio, 1986)

CH = *La Chute* (Folio, 1975)

D = "Discours du 10 décembre 1957" (In *Essais,* Pléiade, 1965)

E = *L'Etranger* (Folio, 1980)

EE = *L'Envers et l'endroit* (Folio "Essais," 1986)

ER = *L'Exil et le royaume* (Folio, 1974)

HR = *L'Homme révolté* (Folio "Essais," 1987)

MS = *Le Mythe de Sisyphe* (Folio "Essais," 1986)

N = *Noces,* suivi de *L'Eté* (Folio, 1986)

P = *La Peste* (Folio, 1974)

RT = "Retour à Tipasa" (In *Noces,* suivi de *L'Eté*)

V = "Ni Victimes ni bourreaux" (In *Actuelles,* "Idées," 1977)

1913, November 7: Birth of Albert Camus in Mondavi, Algeria.

1914, October 11: Death of Lucien Auguste Camus, father of Albert, at the Battle of the Marne in France.

1914–1918: World War I

1918–1923: Camus's intellectual talents recognized by his elementary school teacher, Louis Germain. Camus will dedicate one of his Nobel Prize lectures to Germain, in 1957.

1923–1930: Camus a scholarship student at the Algiers *lycée* (secondary school).

1928–1930: Camus is goalie for the Algiers "Racing-Club" soccer team.

1930: First attacks of tuberculosis. Camus will suffer from this disease the rest of his life.

1932: Camus studies literature and philosophy at the University of Algiers and is influenced by one of his professors, Jean Grenier, author of *Les Iles* (*The Islands*) and advocate of "Mediterranean culture."

1933: Hitler comes to power in Germany. Camus joins an anti-Fascist organization in Algiers.

1934: First marriage of Camus—to Simone Hié. Marriage breaks up two years later.

1934–1937: Years of Camus's involvement with the Communist Party and with the Théâtre du Travail (Workers' Theater). Popular Front in power in

France as of 1936; increasing ideological tensions in Europe.

1937: Publication of *L'Envers et l'endroit* (*The Wrong Side and the Right Side*).

1939: Publication of *Noces* (*Nuptials*). Beginning of World War II.

1940: Camus marries Francine Faure, a native of Oran.

1942–1945: Camus in France until the Liberation. Publication of *L'Etranger* (*The Stranger*), *Le Mythe de Sisyphe* (*The Myth of Sisyphus*), *Le Malentendu* (*The Misunderstanding*) and *Caligula*. Camus meets Sartre in 1944 and associates with the group surrounding Sartre, but declares himself a non-existentialist from the very beginning.

1946–1949: Cultural visits to the United States and South America. Camus leaves the staff of the journal *Combat* in 1947, after having written numerous articles in its pages during and just after the period of the Resistance. Publication of *La Peste* (*The Plague*) in 1947: a major popular success.

1951: Publication of *L'Homme révolté* (*The Rebel*). Beginning of controversy and ultimate split with Sartre.

1952–1955: Publication of *L'Eté* (*Summer*) in 1954. Otherwise, very little original literary activity. By critical consensus, Camus in a state of depression.

1956: Discouraging trip to Algiers in January. Camus's compromise position on the Algerian conflict seems increasingly unrealistic. Publication of *La Chute* (*The Fall*).

1957: Publication of *L'Exil et le royaume* (*Exile and the Kingdom*). On October 17, Camus receives the Nobel Prize in Literature.

1958: Publication of *Actuelles III: Chroniques algériennes,* a series of essays by Camus on the Algerian situation. This volume will be ignored by the press and the critics. Re-edition of *The Wrong Side and the Right Side,* with an important preface by the author.

1959: Several theatrical projects, but also beginning of active and productive writing of *Le Premier homme* (The First Man), an unfinished manuscript that was to be a long semi-autobiographical novel describing the coming-of-age of a young man in Algeria.

1960: January 4: Death of Albert Camus in an automobile accident.

Career Summary

Albert Camus was born in Mondavi, Algeria, on November 7, 1913. His father, Lucien, died of a wound received during the battle of the Marne in the early months of World War I, less than one year after his son's birth. This turn of events meant the end of an independent life for Albert's mother, Catherine, who was obliged, for financial reasons, to move with her children into the small apartment of her mother in working-class Algiers. It was in this district, called Belcourt, that Albert lived until he was seventeen years old.

From age seven until graduation from the *lycée* (secondary school), Camus pursued his studies on a full government scholarship. His intellectual talents were first discovered by an elementary school teacher, Louis Germain, who recognized in his pupil the capacity for original thinking and creative expression. As Camus attained the final years of the *lycée* curriculum, Jean Grenier was the professor who exerted the greatest influence on his thinking, not only in the classroom, but also through his role as active mentor. The author of a book entitled *Les Iles* (1933), Grenier believed in the unity of the Mediterranean culture—that culture centered in Athens and Rome but also including Spain, southern France, and northern Africa. The essential values of Mediterranean culture—harmony of mind and body, clarity of stylistic expression, and a strong sense of moral responsibility—were to permeate Camus's literary works from the very beginning.

1

Camus's first two published works, *L'Envers et l'endroit* (*The Wrong Side and the Right Side,* 1937) and *Noces* (*Nuptials,* 1938), reached only a small readership in Algeria. When they were reprinted in France nearly twenty years later, however, it became clear that each of these volumes contained major themes and imagery that would emerge in more fully developed form in Camus's later, more polished texts. From 1934 until 1937, while he was beginning to exercise his literary talent, Camus became progressively involved in the Communist Party. He was one of the principal organizers of the Marxist-inspired Théâtre du Travail (Workers' Theater); it was during this period that he began to display his talent both in acting and directing—a talent that would remain with him throughout his career. After his break with the Communist Party in 1937, Camus worked as a journalist for *Alger Républicain,* an independent left-wing paper, until the eruption of World War II in September 1939.

Camus composed several of his most important works during the war. They include *L'Etranger* (*The Stranger*), *Le Mythe de Sisyphe* (*The Myth of Sisyphus*), *Caligula, Le Malentendu* (*The Misunderstanding*), and *La Peste* (*The Plague*). When *The Stranger* was printed, in 1942, Camus immediately attained some notoriety among French intellectuals; but it was the great popular success of *The Plague,* finally published in 1947, that assured him a following among the general public. Having received a major literary prize for *The Plague* and having been honored by the French government with a Resistance Medal for his activity during the war, Camus became a major public figure in the political and literary life of France.

2

Throughout the war and until 1951, Camus had been working on a long and ambitious essay entitled *L'Homme révolté* (*The Rebel*). When it appeared on the Parisian intellectual scene, it immediately became the subject of controversy, and received an acerbic negative review in *Les Temps Modernes,* the influential journal edited by the existentialist philosopher Jean-Paul Sartre. Distressed by the poor reception of a work that he considered to be essential to the entirety of his literary production, Camus published no important creative texts for five years. Then, in 1956 appeared *La Chute* (*The Fall*), a short novel of great stylistic rigor and originality, which, along with the subsequent series of short stories entitled *L'Exil et le royaume* (*Exile and the Kingdom*) (1957), helped reestablish Camus's literary reputation, but only partially.

On October 16, 1957 Camus received the Nobel Prize in Literature. Although this should have been a gratifying moment, Camus found himself attacked in the French press as a writer who had not lived up to his promise, who had achieved no major success after *The Plague*. Upon his return to France after the Nobel awards ceremony, Camus bought a home in Lourmarin, a small town in the south of the country where he decided to escape the relentless scrutiny of the press and begin work on a novel to be called *Le Premier homme* (The First Man). He had completed some 80,000 words of this volume in draft form when he was killed in an automobile accident on January 4, 1960, at the age of 46.

CHAPTER ONE

Reading Albert Camus

Although the works for which Camus is most famous are either fictional or philosophical in mode, and therefore removed from the immediacy of everyday experience, nevertheless it is important for the reader of his texts to be acquainted with the cultural and social factors that played a determining role in his life and in his development as an artist. Once we have an idea of the place in which he lived—its geography, its history, its political ideologies—we may hope to gain access more readily to the author's personality and to his thoughts on the place of the artist in contemporary society. Before analyzing any particular work of Camus, therefore, I propose that we examine the importance of Camus's homeland, Algeria; the elements in Camus's personality that informed not only his code of ethics and political engagement, but also his conception of the possibilities and limitations of artistic endeavor; his philosophical or theoretical views of literary creation; and some of the concrete forms and techniques he developed over the years to express his thoughts with a subtle combination of clarity, economy, and force.

Algeria

The country we now call Algeria has a rich and complex past. Used by the Phoenicians as a convenient

4

base of operations for commercial ventures, the country was colonized successively by Carthaginians, Romans, Moslems, Turks, and the French. The period of French domination extended from 1830 until the independence of Algeria in 1962, two years after the death of Albert Camus. While Camus lived in the capital city of Algiers during his childhood and youth, the Arab majority began gradually to resent its political and legal second-class status, its enforced subservience to the predominantly Christian and white French colonialists (called *pieds noirs,* or "black feet" because of the black shoes they wore). While the French and the Arabs moved inexorably toward open hostility in the major coastline cities, the Berber nomad population suffered extreme poverty and privation in the outlying mountain regions. Growing up in the working class neighborhood of Belcourt, in which French and Arabs came into daily contact and where mosques and churches were not far removed from each other, Camus developed an acute sensitivity to problems of race, class, language, religion, and territory. His world was a delicately balanced one consisting of heterogeneous elements vying with each other for recognition and for dominance.

Because Camus grew up among simple people, many of whom were illiterate, and because he witnessed their enduring dignity through periods of material hardship, hunger, and physical suffering, he retained throughout his career a strong sense of empathy for those people whose lives were consumed by unremitting labor, whose aspirations rarely were fulfilled. This empathy underlies his political positions and informs substantial parts of his literary works; it also helps to explain why Camus never felt comfortable among the privileged, why he never felt at home in the status-conscious world of the Parisian intelligentsia.

The American reader of Camus will find many of the author's writings highly political. The long philosophical essay entitled *The Rebel* (which we shall examine in Chapter Five of this book), for example, cannot be understood in isolation, but needs to be viewed within the political debates of the period we once called the Cold War. And all of Camus's voluminous journalistic essays on the Algerian problem constitute what the French call *prises de position:* position-taking on issues whose parameters are defined by the ideologies that dominate society at a given moment. But Camus's political consciousness emerged naturally from his life in Belcourt and from the investigative journalism he initiated in Algiers, in Oran, and in the mountain retreats of the Berber tribesmen. It was impossible for Camus not to write politically; when he saw suffering and injustice, he always sought out the cause of these evils, and most often found that cause embedded in (and implicitly justified by) a government or a political ideology.

As we shall see, Camus's greatest strength, his greatest talent, lay in his ability to present moral problems in artistic terms. But it should not be forgotten that these problems usually had a political dimension and that Camus had the courage of his convictions, even when these became unpopular with the leaders of governments and with fellow-artists whose opinions he felt duty-bound to oppose. As we turn briefly to the salient features of Camus's personality, we need to keep in mind that the writer's tastes and sensibility did not evolve in isolation, but against the background of the Algerian cultural milieu—a region he maintained within his memory long after he had departed its geographical reality.

Camus the Person

In interviews and public appearances, when he had become well-known to French readers, Camus often evoked memories of his Algerian childhood to help explain the evolution of his political thought and of his art. During the years immediately following the close of World War II, when many European intellectuals turned toward the dogmatism of radical ideologies, Camus retained a sense of measure and equilibrium in his views that one can trace back to his early experiences in North Africa. Although he and his family and friends knew poverty, they lived in a beautiful and sunny natural environment, close to the sea. Thus poverty did not necessarily imply misery and desperation, at least relatively speaking. It is because he remembered not only a small apartment with no running water or electricity, but also days spent on the seashore and in the hills overlooking Algiers when the blue of the sky merged with the blue of the ocean, that Camus was not disposed to share the stark pessimism of those of his contemporaries who saw humankind imprisoned in a dark world from which there was no escape. Camus was no naive idealist, and he understood, because he had witnessed it, the brutal evil of which human beings are capable. But in the midst of the greatest violence and suffering, he found reason to hope that men and women would not destroy the world

7

precisely because this world in which we live is both beautiful and fragile. As we shall see, some of Camus's earliest writings amounted to lyrical hymns to Nature that seem, on the surface, to be far removed from the tragic intensity of his mature texts. Yet even in the bleak world of *The Plague,* as we shall see, the two main characters manage to put death and misery behind them when they join in a fraternal plunge into the protective embrace of the ocean.

When Camus looked back on his early days, and when he would occasionally write about them after having attained celebrity, he emphasized two essential interrelated themes: silence and simplicity. Camus's mother was illiterate and partially deaf. Because of her ability to read lips, she and her son could communicate at a very low level of sound. Camus grew up in a household in which words, because they were exchanged so seldom, had great value. One finds in Camus's literary works a similar emphasis on the possibility of communication with few or no words, on the importance of using words with caution and care. When Camus introduces a verbose character, we know we should be on our guard as readers, careful to distinguish what that character is trying to hide under the mask of his superficial chattiness. The straightforward expository style one finds not only in his essays and journalistic writings, but also in several of his creative prose texts, constitutes an attempt on Camus's part to adhere to that original simplicity that characterized his life before the drastic and dramatic interruptions of certain key personal and historical events.

At age seventeen, Camus contracted tuberculosis. This was the first decisive interruption in his life, the

first disruption of his everyday routine and of his aspirations. Until this time, Camus had enjoyed physical
activity, and had been the star goalie of his soccer
team. The onset of the disease with which he had to
deal henceforth on a regular basis, with painful repeated treatments, changed him in a profound way. In
discovering sickness, he observed, in his own body, a
first absurdity of the human condition: the manner in
which we are all subject to the vagaries of fortune,
good or bad, to what the ancients called Fate. Not only
were Camus's physical activities severely curtailed,
but his disease prohibited him from joining the ranks
of the French civil service: this meant that he could
not become a professor in the state-run educational
system. The postgraduate studies in philosophy in
which Camus was to excel would not lead to a teaching
career. Instead he turned toward journalism as a
means to support himself and to gain experience as a
writer.

The second disruption in Camus's life was not personal but historical: he, like all members of his generation between 1939 and 1945, was caught up in World
War II. After spending the first years of the war in
Oran, Algeria's second-largest city, and after complet-
ing *The Stranger, The Myth of Sisyphus,* and the first
version of *Caligula,* Camus was in need of rest. Having
suffered from an attack of tuberculosis, he went to the
mountainous and isolated region of the Massif Central
in France to convalesce. While Camus was regaining
his strength, the Allies successfully undertook Operation Torch, whereby they wrested North Africa from
the Germans. As of November 7, 1942, Camus was cut
off from his wife and family, who had remained in Al-

geria. Until the end of the war he was to stay in France, where, beginning in 1943, he joined in the Resistance against the German occupation forces. It was during this period that Camus experienced the loneliness of exile—which would become one of the major themes of his major literary works. At the same time, as a member of a Resistance network and as a writer for the anti-Nazi underground newspaper *Combat*, he learned the value of political and social commitment, which the French call *engagement*.

In his personal battle against tuberculosis and in his wartime combat against Nazism, Camus first submitted to, then rebelled against the forces of external necessity. Neither his disease nor the European conflict could be avoided. Camus faced both events with steadfast courage; but each of these disruptions added disorder and cacophony to his central core of silence and simplicity. During the fifteen years separating the end of World War II from his death, as Camus became progressively more involved politically, greatly concerned over the threat of a nuclear conflict and over the uncertain fate of his Algerian homeland, the uncomplicated pleasures of his childhood seemed to be remnants of a lost order rather than elements still available for the construction of a future happiness.

Camus's Theory of Artistic Creation

For Camus, the artist could justify his art only by accepting and living within the contradictions of his time. Since our age is that of monstrous events—of large-scale wars, massive persecution of ethnic minorities, genocide, starvation, uncontrolled proliferating technologies—and since the role of the artist is to bear witness to these events, it is impossible for the creator of works of the imagination to remain isolated in a self-made ivory tower. Although Camus and others of his generation could look back with some nostalgia on a less complicated era, their anguished task consisted in finding a path that might lead to new forms of art appropriate and responsive to the present moment. Unlike Jean-Paul Sartre, the existentialist with whom he was too often compared, Camus never composed a book called *What Is Literature?* and never wrote a systematic treatise to explain his views on the act of writing. Nevertheless, on the occasion of receiving the Nobel Prize, Camus set down in concise form his essential views on the question; from his statements at the awards banquet in the Town Hall of Stockholm and from a talk he gave a few days later at the University of Uppsala we can glean the equivalent of an *art poétique* that will put in perspective some of the major issues raised by his works. Throughout his remarks we will note that he never forgets the lessons of his childhood in Algeria but that he recognizes his fate as a transplanted European subject to the complexities of advanced civilization in the second half of the twentieth century.

In the comments that follow, I shall refer to both the acceptance speech itself (*Discours* of December 10, 1957) and to the Uppsala lecture (*Conférence* of December 14, 1957). Both documents center on the same issues and are characterized by the same subtle combination of somber realism and guarded optimism.

According to Camus, the artist (writer, musician, painter, inventor of fictions in all forms) becomes him-

11

self or "forges his existence" in a back-and-forth movement between his own aspirations, his fundamental love of beauty, and the human community in which he lives and for whom he creates (*D* 1072). The artist experiences this movement as discomfort and conflict, especially when, having attained celebrity, he feels increasing pressure from the community in whose name he works to take clear and unyielding stands on the political and social issues of the day. Thus, when Camus writes that the artist is "torn" between the beauty he knows to exist and the human suffering from which he cannot escape, we must understand that word in all of its force (*D* 1074). As he nears the conclusion of the *Discours,* after noting the necessity of pursuing both the truth and freedom in the creation of art, Camus makes a very revealing admission about himself and about the enduring value of his past experience as it influences his present course of action. He writes:

> I never could renounce the light, the simple happiness of being, the life of freedom I knew as a child. Yet although this nostalgia explains many of my errors and mistakes, it no doubt also helped me to better understand my calling, it helps me still as I stand, blindly, with all those silent men who can endure the life allotted them in this world only by the memory or the return of brief moments of happiness and freedom (*D* 1074; this and all further translations from the French are mine).

We see here Camus's desire to unify past happiness (the image of light taken from the Algerian natural environment) with the present situation, to bring beauty and suffering together in a harmonizing synthesis. When he delivered his speeches in Stockholm and Uppsala, Camus had just completed his last volume of short stories, entitled *L'Exil et le royaume* (*Exile and the Kingdom*). As we shall see in Chapter Six of this book, each of the stories included in the collection constitutes an attempt to find a balance between the condition of exile or abandonment shared by all people and the domain of beauty or perfection (symbolized by the word "Kingdom") which the artist wishes to inhabit. The synthesis that Camus suggests fleetingly in the closing moments of the *Discours* is the aesthetic *and* moral goal toward which his final short stories struggle.

In the *Conférence* set forth in Uppsala (and originally delivered under the general title "L'Artiste et son temps"—[The Artist and his Times]), Camus organizes his remarks around a question that he repeats on several occasions in the development of his argument: "L'art est-il un luxe mensonger?" (Is art a deceitful luxury?). Camus attempts to demonstrate that the creative act is not sufficient unto itself (he opposes the doctrine of *l'art pour l'art*), but that it is also not to be confused with mere mimicry or the superficial reproduction of the objective world (in this he opposes the adherents of Socialist Realism who dominated the literary scene in many Marxist Eastern-bloc countries). According to Camus, the essential goal of all art is to communicate clearly by concrete rather than unnecessarily abstract or formalistic constructs, thereby creating a bridge between the expressiveness of the individual creator and the mute conscience of the public. Works of the imagination reside within our world yet cannot express mere acquiescence to the status

13

quo. Once again, Camus sees the artist delicately balanced between two extreme positions—in this case, between revolt and assent:

In a certain sense, art is a revolt against the world and its fugitive, unfinished qualities: the function of artistic endeavor is to give another form to a reality that it must nevertheless conserve because this reality is the source of its emotional power. In this regard everyone and no one is a realist. Art is neither the total refusal of nor the total assent to what is. Art is at the same time refusal (revolt) and assent (acquiescence), which is why it can only be a perpetually renewed anguish (*déchirement:* literally, a "tearing-apart") (*C* 1090).

What Camus proposes here is a theory of art as *tension,* in which the sought-for balancing of opposites occurs only with great difficulty, only at the expense of the artist's inner peace. The synthesis of which Camus wrote in the *Discours* remains the fundamental goal of his work, but the *Conférence* underlines the precariousness of the balancing act itself and warns against excessive optimism. Camus asserts that the world in which we live needs art more than ever, but the producing and forming process whereby reality is transmuted into an imaginary equivalent is a highly problematic labor, full of risks for the individual who is drawn simultaneously to the exigencies of the world and the alchemy of the word.

Camus and the Elaboration of Literary Form

Camus did not begin his career as a writer with a theoretical view of literature. It is only after he had composed several important and well-received works that he began, first in his *Carnets* (*Notebooks*), then in essays and articles, to reflect in a methodical way on the act of writing. If we are to understand Camus, therefore understand the evolution of his conception of literature, we must read his major texts in sequence, thereby observing not only the variety of themes and ideas they contain, but also the diversity of their formal construction. When he gave his talks in Stockholm and Uppsala, Camus could look back over twenty years of published writings and draw conclusions from a convenient retrospective point of view. When he began to create, however, like most writers of imaginative prose, he was groping for a personal style; this style did not emerge immediately or easily, and one can say that even in his later years, when he had attained a certain technical mastery, he never stopped experimenting with new forms.

If we survey the entirety of Camus's writings, we note that he was most successful in the genres of the novel, the short story, the philosophical essay, and the drama. Although he wrote some poetry at the very beginning of his career, he never excelled in this genre, preferring to remain an enlightened admirer of his most talented contemporaries: he had the greatest respect for René Char, with whom he corresponded regularly and who exerted a strong influence on *L'Homme révolté* (*The Rebel*). As mentioned, Camus was a journalist, in Algeria and in France, before and after World War II. For a full comprehension of Camus's political views it would be necessary to study his journalistic work in some detail, but that is beyond the scope of this book. For our purposes, I shall allude occasionally to his newspaper articles and interviews, but only insofar as they illuminate his principal texts, which are either literary or philosophical.

In the chapters that follow I shall discuss individual works by Camus considered by critics and by the general reading public to be his most powerful and compelling. To analyze the major texts in some detail I have had to eliminate some others from consideration. Admirers of Camus's theater will be disappointed to find that I analyze only *Caligula* in a systematic way, and that I devote little space to *Le Malentendu* and *Les Justes*. It is true that Camus was a passionate man of the theater, as writer, director, and even actor. His stage adaptation of William Faulkner's *Requiem for a Nun* was brilliant and enjoyed prolonged success in Paris. His adaptations of Calderón and Dostoevsky were substantial literary achievements as well. And it is also true that near the end of his life Camus contemplated purchasing a theater of his own over which he could exercise artistic control and ensure the production of the best in contemporary plays. All this notwithstanding, it must be said that Camus's own plays are no longer performed, even in France, with any regularity. Most of them appear excessively verbose to today's audiences; most seem to consist in a theatrical exposition of what are essentially moral or philosophical problems, where the staging remains secondary to the ideas expressed by the characters. The one exception to this tendency is *Caligula,* which retains a central position within Camus's literary production and which lends itself to imaginative interpretation.

In order to accomplish the double goal of tracing the

evolution of Camus's thought and highlighting the formal diversity of his texts, I have decided to proceed chronologically, beginning with his two earliest published volumes, *L'Envers et l'endroit* (*The Wrong Side and the Right Side*) and *Noces* (*Nuptials*) and ending with *L'Exil et le royaume* (*Exile and the Kingdom*) and *L'Eté* (*Summer*). In each chapter I shall analyze two works that were composed at approximately the same time but that exhibit contrasting generic, formal or structural features. Thus, in Chapter Two I shall discuss a series of short stories (*The Wrong Side and the Right Side*) and a group of lyrical essays (*Nuptials*); in Chapter Three, a short novel (*L'Etranger*) (*The Stranger*) and a philosopical essay (*Le Mythe de Sisyphe*) (*The Myth of Sisyphus*); in Chapter Four, a play (*Caligula*) and a longer novel (*La Peste*) (*The Plague*); in Chapter Five, a second philosophical essay (*L'Homme révolté*) (*The Rebel*) and a short ironical novel (*La Chute*) (*The Fall*); and in Chapter Six, a series of short stories (*Exile and the Kingdom*) and a final group of lyrical essays (*Summer*). My purpose in establishing these juxtapositions is to indicate that art, for Camus, was always essentially a matter of form, and that the expression of ideas, however abstract or difficult, could never be separated from the form in which they are enveloped. It is not a matter of indifference that *The Stranger* is a short novel told in the first person using a specific form of the French past tense called the *passé composé;* and it is crucial to the message of *The Fall* that the plot or action of its pages be staged in the form of a highly theatrical monologue. Although academically trained in philosophy, Camus, unlike Sartre, did not write philosophical treatises. At the same time, he did not shy away from issues that deserve to be called philosophical; yet in treating these issues, he sought for varied means of expression, preferring the essay, the novel, the theater, to systematic or objective modes of exposition.

Camus thought of the contemporary artist as the creator of myths that are both challenging and accessible to the public. As we proceed in our reading of his individual works, we shall attempt to discover the thematic continuities of these myths as they evolve over time and as they assume a variegated succession of masks.

L'Envers et l'endroit (*The Wrong Side and the Right Side*) and *Noces* (*Nuptials*)

In the year in which he received the Nobel Prize, Camus was prompted to look back over the first twenty years of his literary career. Although he had become well-known in France both for his prose fictions and for his journalistic *engagement,* many of his faithful readers wished to gain a clear understanding of his development as an artist, which could be possible only if Camus were willing to republish his two earliest creative works that had been written between 1936 and 1938: *The Wrong Side and the Right Side,* and *Nuptials.* These texts had appeared in very limited editions in Algeria, and had become expensive collectors' items by the late fifties. Despite some hesitations, Camus acceded to the wishes of his readers and the books came out in 1957 and 1958.

Both short texts are important not only because they foreshadow many of the major themes of Camus's later works, but also in their own right. At age twenty-two, the future author of *The Stranger* and *The Plague* was already a gifted, if occasionally awkward, writer. His sensitivity to his natural surroundings and to the hard-working people around him was already evident, and he was already experimenting, often successfully, with narrative technique. In the meditative preface that he wrote for *The Wrong Side and the Right Side* in 1957, Camus insisted that, despite some formal shortcomings, this series of essays had value as a testimony (*témoignage*): in it, if we read carefully, we will discover what the author calls the single source (*source unique*) of his artistic endeavor (*EE* 12-13). Much of what Camus writes in his preface concerns the Parisian literary scene and its rigorous demands on his time, the difficulty he has accepting compliments gracefully, his feeling that this world of masks and poses does not correspond to the difficult inner essence of art: or, as he puts it in ultimate simplicity, "ce n'est pas cela" ("that is not it," "that begs the important question"). In rereading his early essays, however, Camus is gratified to rediscover, at the very origins of his activity as writer, certain key images that do *not* beg the large questions:

> rereading *The Wrong Side and the Right Side* after so many years, for this [new] edition, I know instinctively as I look at certain pages, and despite the awkwardness, that this is it [*que c'est cela*]. *Cela,* that is to say this old woman, a silent mother, poverty, the light on the Italian olive trees, love silent yet shared, all those things that in my eyes bear witness to the truth (*EE* 25).

As we turn, first to *The Wrong Side and the Right Side,* then to *Nuptials,* we shall look for those elements, both formal and thematic, that transcend the technical limitations of the twenty-two-year-old writer and that seem to "bear witness to the truth."

I. *The Wrong Side and the Right Side*

Camus's first published work is composed of five short stories or essays, each of which has a distinctive tone and its own individual narrative unity. Although one senses that the author would like the reader to view his stories as fictitious, a strong personal coloration emerges from numerous passages: indeed, given knowledge of Camus's life, it is easy enough to demonstrate that several of the most compelling anecdotes are taken directly from the writer's experiences as a child and adolescent. It is significant, therefore, that all five stories are told in the first person. At the same time, however, it would be an oversimplification to reduce what Camus writes to mere confessional autobiography. In fact, in differing ways, each story is constructed on a balancing of the particular (the events related by the narrator, the anecdotal content of his activity) and the universal (the moral reflections made by the narrator once the related events have been examined for their deep significance). Each of the five narratives combines the techniques of the short story and the essay; it is the hybridization of these two forms, more typical of seventeenth- and eighteenth-century French *moralisme* than of the modern age, that lends Camus's early volume its curious yet original flavor.

1. "L'Ironie" ("Irony")

The first of the narratives, entitled "Irony," combines three apparently disparate strands into one final generalizing reflection on the part of the first-person

21

moralizing narrator. In the first and simplest of the vignettes, a young man who is sensitive to the solitude and suffering of an old woman abandons her to follow his friends to the cinema. As he leaves the apartment in which she lives, he notes that the light in her window goes out: in an important sense, at least in his judgment, it is he who has condemned her to darkness. In the second anecdote, the narrator describes a garrulous and tiresome old man who imposes himself on younger people, wishing to be at the center of conversation. Yet the narrator notes that this forced sociability is in reality the mask of the man's loneliness and impending death. The "irony" of the story's title derives from the old man's refusal to see the "irony" in the eyes of the young men who listen to his endless tales without sympathy (*EE 42*). Thus for Camus the notion of irony as such is coupled with abandonment and cruelty. What the young men cannot understand is that they too will grow old, that they too are subject to the laws of mortality; their immaturity consists in not showing sympathy toward a person who, after all, merely mirrors their own existential predicament. In the third vignette, which contains unmistakable autobiographical elements, the narrator describes (in this exceptional case, from a thinly veiled third-person perspective) a large family living in cramped surroundings and dominated by an overbearing grandmother. The grandmother spends much of her time complaining about her physical ailments, acting out the drama of her affliction in such an overtly theatrical way that, progressively, the family becomes numb to her appeals for sympathy. She dies after great (and real) suffering; and it is only on the day of her burial that her grandson (transparently a figure of Camus himself) feels grief. The third narrative strand ends with a description of the sun's rays in winter falling on the bay the cemetery overlooks.

At the end of the story, in one concise paragraph, the narrator addresses the crucial question of the unity of his fiction. How, precisely, can the three strands be woven together? The reader of the text will have already noted one theme common to each anecdote: that of aging and its attendant solitude. It does seem remarkable that a young writer should be so fascinated by such a theme, so capable of empathy for the old; in these early pages we see a first indication of what will become Camus's constant obsession with death and dying, with the importance of accepting the conditions of one's mortality as a first step toward living an authentic life. The primary meaning of the story does not end here, however. In his concluding comments, the narrator places on one side of a scale or balance the abandoned woman, the ignored old man, and the "useless" death of the grandmother, but on the other ("on the other side"—*de l'autre côté*) he evokes *la lumière du monde* ("the light of the world") (*EE 52*). This is the same light that appeared in the cemetery at the end of the third vignette. Although Camus does not make his symbolism straightforward or univocal, one senses that this light, whose role is to counterbalance human suffering and inevitable death, is that force of nature which permeates life and grants it meaningfulness. Light symbolism will pervade Camus's literary works, not always in this guise, but it will always be associated with a certain powerful inevitability guiding human destiny. As we move now to the second story in

23

the collection, we need to keep in mind the delicate balancing of human suffering and what Camus chooses to call *la lumière du monde*.

2. "Entre Oui et Non" ("Between Yes and No")

The central subject of this story is the love of the narrator for his mother—a love whose strength is evident despite the near-muteness of both characters. Here, we recognize the family situation of Camus rendered in undisguised form, certain details in the text having been borrowed from his childhood experience and memories. What makes the story most interesting, however, is the technique used by the narrator, which consists of weaving together three temporal levels or "layers." First, there is the narrative present: the teller of the story, who is also its protagonist, is seated in a café in the Arab section of Algiers as the evening begins. He describes his physical surroundings, the smells, sights and sounds that characterize this exotic environment, and evokes the beauty of the sea and stars beyond the café's open doors and windows. Second, there is the narrative past: from the beginning of the story, we understand that the Arab establishment is essentially a frame for the recollections of the protagonist, whose mind constantly drifts back to his childhood. The reader finds himself moving from one level to the other with the regularity of a pendulum swing, but the movement is so rapid that one occasionally loses one's balance. In the final paragraph, the narrator himself wonders: "But at this moment, where am I? And how can I separate this deserted café from the remembered room of my past?" (*EE 71*). The third narrative level is that of the timeless moralizing voice of the speaker, whose reflections on the unifying force of memory introduce the story and anchor its anecdotal material in a rigorous, if somewhat cryptic, meditation on the relation of time to human happiness. For the young Camus, the act of remembering does not take place with the pseudo-objectivity of a photograph, but is a highly subjective reordering of the fragments that compose our past and our identity. In introducing this third narrative level, Camus makes it possible for the reader to move beyond the confines of the story's related events, toward a higher level of analytical or theoretical abstraction. The first two pages of "Between Yes and No" establish the thematic focus of the subsequent alternations between present and past.

In this introductory section, Camus describes the way in which he is able to retrieve, from the depths of forgetfulness, "the intact remembrance of a pure emotion, of an instant suspended in eternity" (*EE 55*). The act of remembering silences all irony and is the equivalent of a "repatriation" or return home (*Ibid.*). Camus uses the terms *patrie* and *rapatriement* in implicit contradistinction to the notion of exile or estrangement: memory makes it possible for the individual consciousness to return from its lostness or exiled condition within the world and to find its proper or appointed place. As we shall see in Chapter Six of this book, this opposition between native land (*patrie*) or "kingdom" (*royaume*) and exile (*exil*) is the unifying tension of Camus's last major creative work. The same opposition emerges already in *The Wrong Side and the Right Side,* but less explicitly, in muted form. Readers of twentieth-century French literature will note in

Camus's evocation of the power of memory to recover the essence of the past from the slightest of sense impressions an unmistakable reference to Marcel Proust, the author of *A la recherche du temps perdu* (*Remembrance of Things Past*). According to Camus, and following Proust's theories, apparently insignificant phenomena in the exterior world are related in a fundamental way to the emotions that organize and control the depth of our inner life. Thus, Camus writes:

> We love the gracefulness of a gesture, the chance appearance of a tree in the landscape. And to recreate all this love, we possess only a detail, but which suffices: the smell of a room shut for too long, the singular sound of a footstep on the road (*EE 55–56*).

In "Between Yes and No" Camus will forge links between the sense impressions of the narrative present (the evening in the Arab café) and the love he feels for his mother—a love that resonates beneath all his current sentiments.

If we turn to the first narrative level—the account of the young man's past—we find very little in the way of plot or action. Very little happens here: Camus seems content to sketch in broad strokes certain typical scenes from a modest Algerian childhood, some of which are recognizably from his own personal experience. The one exception to this rule occurs when the narrator recounts the evening in which his mother, sitting on the balcony, somnolent after a day of work, is brutally attacked by an unknown assailant who has managed to enter and depart her apartment in silence. On advice from the doctor who has examined his mother after the incident, the young man spends the night with her, sleeping next to her in her bed, listening to her weep as she relives the attack in her dreams. Thinking back on this episode from his present-day perspective, the narrator speaks of the solidarity he feels with his mother, and asserts that his memory was able to bring back from these moments of horror, followed by close emotional communion, "the image, both distressing and tender, of a mutual solitude (*solitude à deux*)" (*EE 65*).

Central to the meaning of the story is its tone, which requires some explanation. What Camus calls *solitude à deux* should not be confused with loneliness or alienation; on the contrary, this type of "solitude" in which two people discover each other's love beyond or below the level of words constitutes an ideal state for the author, a state of things that one can recover only rarely, through the power of memory, and that otherwise merely stands as a distant reminder of the happiness we have lost in the routine and distractions of our present everyday existence. Another expression similar to this shared and mute "solitude" is that of "indifference"—a term the narrator uses to describe both the verbally inexpressible affection of his mother (*EE 63*) and the ineffable beauty of the bay and its lights outside the Arab café (*EE 71*). As we shall see when we attempt to understand the concluding pages of *The Stranger,* for Camus the word "indifference" does not hold negative connotations, and is usually associated with love or tenderness.

Although "Between Yes and No" does not have the thematic richness or complexity of thought that characterize his later fictional works, it is certainly one of the most important of Camus's early stories, in that it makes very effective use of temporal alternations to establish the centrality of what the author himself calls "the transparence and the simplicity of a lost paradise." In the following passage, we will recognize the contextual meaning of this transparence as well as the title of the story:

If tonight it is the image of a certain childhood that comes back to me, how can I not welcome the lesson of love and of poverty that it contains? Since this hour is like an interval between yes and no, I leave for other hours the hope or the loathing of life. Yes, to gather and preserve the transparence and the simplicity of a lost paradise: in an image (*EE 68*).

Just as "Irony" was based on a balancing between human suffering and "the light of the world," in "Between Yes and No" Camus delineates an opposition between those moments of existential decision-making (saying yes *or* no, finding hope *or* loathing for life) and those other moments of poetic meditation and of suspended time (*between* yes and no) in which it becomes possible to recover transparence and simplicity. Neither of the two opposed terms can entirely dominate or cancel out the other; both are necessary, and it is their active conflict that lies at the source, not only of this particular story, but also of Camus's own career tensions, as he attempted to combine overt journalistic investigation of the misery of the world with the quiet introspection of literary creation.

3. "La Mort dans l'âme" ("Death in the Soul")

In the summer of 1936, as Léon Blum and the left-coalition Popular Front took power in France and as

Nazism continued its ascendancy in Germany, Camus departed for summer holiday in Central Europe with his wife Simone and his good friend Yves Bourgeois. It was during this trip that Camus made two important discoveries: first, he learned by opening a letter addressed to his wife that she had begun to be addicted to drugs; and second, as he observed the changing scenery and varied civilizations of the Continent, he began to take notes that would later be used in his early literary works. The Central Europe trip was thus a time of personal crisis (his marriage never recovered from the revelation of Simone's drug dependency, and was later to be dissolved) during which Camus was brought face to face with the limitations of his love and with his aspirations as beginning artist. The third and central story of *The Wrong Side and the Right Side,* entitled "Death in the Soul," is a slightly transposed account of the days Camus spent alone in Prague, Czechoslovakia, while Simone and Yves continued their travels together by kayak (because of his tuberculosis, Camus could not take the strain of the kayaking; some literary-critic detectives have made much of Simone and Yves as a "couple," but there is nothing to substantiate after-the-fact rumors of this kind).

"Death in the Soul" is perhaps the most successful of the stories collected in *The Wrong Side and the Right Side;* certainly it is the most quoted by readers of Camus. There are two essential reasons for this success: (1) in describing his feelings of loneliness and estrangement in a city whose language and customs he does not understand, Camus is relating an experience many travelers have, and is communicating quite directly to the reader, who can empathize with the thoughts of the narrator; (2) at the same time, in addressing the issues of solitude and alienation, the narrator formulates his analysis in the terms and with the fervor of existential anguish. We sense, underneath the prose of Camus, echoes of Dostoevsky and Kierkegaard, a certain resonance emanating from the author's formal training in philosophy. What Camus evokes in "Death in the Soul" is not loneliness as a mere pretext for self-pity or for Romantic effusion, but loneliness as a way of being in the world, as the necessary precondition for understanding existence.

"Death in the Soul" is divided into three parts. First is the narrator/protagonist's account of his stay in Prague before the arrival of his friends. Second is his description of the continuation of his travels, in the company of his friends, through the countryside of Silesia and Moravia, to Vienna, and finally, to Italy. In the third and final section, the narrator compares his experiences in Prague to his sentiments in Italy, and attempts to define the fundamental characteristics of each place, the differing ways in which each of these geographical/cultural entities impinges on his imagination and causes him to search for the significance of his life.

In the first section, the protagonist attempts to organize himself, to create a routine. By waking up at a certain hour, by eating at the same restaurant, by visiting churches and other monuments to the city's past, he defends himself against the anguish that threatens to overwhelm him. He realizes, however, that his efforts to seek comfort either in habitual actions or in the contemplation of works of art are doomed to ultimate failure. As soon as he departs the cathedral or museum that has momentarily held him captive, he is left to his own devices once again, he remains a stranger:

> Churches, palaces and museums, I tried to alleviate my anguish in all works of art. A classic manoeuvre: I wanted to convert my revolt into melancholy. But in vain. As soon as I left these places, I was a stranger [a foreigner: *un étranger*] (*EE 80–81*).

In this passage Camus exploits the double meaning of the word *étranger,* as he will, to maximum effect, in his novel of that title. The protagonist of "Death in the Soul" is a stranger in Prague because he is a foreigner, because the customs of the city are foreign to him. Yet just as in *The Stranger* we sense that Meursault's actions are significant precisely insofar as they deviate from the norms established by society, in the same way in "Death in the Soul" we understand that the experience of foreignness or cultural difference constitutes the emotional state of mind that allows the protagonist to come face-to-face with himself.

The Prague section of the story culminates with an event that disturbs the protagonist's tenuously established sense of routine. In a room next to his own, the hotel personnel discover a man who has recently died. In the narrator's words, we see

> the shadow of a dead man stretched out on the bed and that of a policeman guarding the body. The two shadows intersected at a right angle. This light upset me. It was authentic, the real light of a life, of a lived afternoon, a light that makes one see one's own life (*EE 85*).

31

As the narrator proceeds with his own story, with the continuation of his travels, with reflections on what he calls the death that resides within the "soul," this real death will remain in the background as the source that gives light to his thoughts. What will preoccupy the narrator until the end of his tale is the fact that the unknown man's death occurred in silence, while other people were going about their everyday activity, while he (the protagonist) was reading the advertisement on his shaving cream. This disparity between significant event and insignificant everydayness is what Camus will later call "the absurd" (*l'absurde*).

In the second section of "Death in the Soul," the narrator describes in lyrical terms his love of Italy, and especially of the area surrounding Vicenza. Here he finds that "every person encountered, every smell of the street, all serves as pretext for measureless love" (*EE 90*). Once again, as in "Between Yes and No," Camus speaks of the tender indifference of nature (*EE 91*), and stresses the interdependence of his thoughts and of the physical environment. Thus it would seem, on the surface, that Italy represents the polar opposite of Prague, the location in which the protagonist is no longer a stranger or foreigner, but in which he rediscovers "the lesson of the sun and of my native land" (*EE 92*).

In the third section of the story, the narrator attempts to explain why the apparent differences between the two places can be resolved into a higher synthesis. In fact, if he loves the Italian countryside, it is not because of its richness or fullness, but rather because of what Camus calls its "nothingness." And this nothingness, this void, communicates in an essential way with his sense of anguish:

> And in these fields whirling under the sun's rays and in the dust, in these shaved hills crusty with burned grass, I could touch with my finger the spare and featureless form of the taste for nothingness that I carried within myself. This country [Italy] brought me back to the center of my being and placed me opposite my secret anguish (*EE 93*).

Prague and Vicenza are not exactly the same: Prague is the place in which anguish flourishes; Vicenza is the place in which the savage but indifferent beauty of nature forces human consciousness to face that anguish. In the end, the narrator refuses to choose between the two locations (which are, of course, two parts of his "soul"), but asserts their equal importance. His principal allegiance, like that of Camus the person, is to the Mediterranean culture, to those lands flooded in sunlight that witnessed the beginnings of Western civilization. Yet he realizes that the stark encounter with death in Prague had its own illumination, its own darker light to shed on the search for meaning that has become his life.

4. "Amour de vivre" ("Love of Life")

Like "Death in the Soul," "Love of Life" is based on a short trip Camus himself made—in this case, to the Balearic Islands located off the Mediterranean coast of Spain. The narrator of the story speaks specifically of Palma, the principal city of the island of Majorca, and of another island in the group called Ibiza. This collection of islands today forms a province of Spain, and its monuments include vestiges from earlier con-quering peoples—notably the Romans and the Arabs. Camus chooses the Balearics as a privileged site for a meditation on the virtues of travel, or more precisely, what the French call *dépaysement* (literally, the sense of uprooting or "loss of one's homeland"); and in the course of this meditation, he reflects on the meaning of Mediterranean culture.

Readers of "Death in the Soul" may be somewhat disappointed in "Love of Life," which merely repeats the major themes of the previous story but in a more direct, more transparent way. When the narrator of "Love of Life" tells us that the essential worth of travel lies in its disruption of routine, when he asserts that travel, in removing the masks we assume in our native culture, causes us to examine who we are, we recognize the same network of concerns that had organized "Death in the Soul." Similarly, when, at the end of the story, he speaks of the "nothingness" of the Mediterra-nean landscape using the Spanish word *Nada* (*EE 107*), we once again recognize a theme from the earlier tale.

The power of "Love of Life" resides less in its explicit themes than in its capacity to evoke an atmosphere and an exalted state of mind. In the first section of the story, the narrator describes his experience one eve-ning in a small café in Palma, when he, surrounded and hemmed in by a crowd of men, witnesses a young woman's erotic dance. The woman is not beautiful, her appeal is not based on fineness of feature or proportion, but rather on her ability to mime the act of love with consummate skill. The narrator compares her to "a vile goddess emerging from the water" (*EE 102*), no

34

doubt alluding to the Greek myth of Aphrodite's birth from the waves, but transforming the goddess of beauty into an emblem of animal sexuality. Although his depiction of her might seem realistic to the point of cruelty, the narrator writes that "she was the ignoble and exalting image of life" (*Ibid.*). It is this coupling of the ignoble and the exalting that characterizes the tone of the passage as a whole. Readers of nineteenth-century French literature may recall a similar coupling in the works of Emile Zola (the descriptions of love in its physicality in *Germinal,* for example), whom Camus resembles here as he evokes erotic desire within the framework of the meeting-ground of the lower classes.

"Love of Life" is composed of quieter moments as well, moments in which the protagonist merges with the surrounding landscape to such an extent that he loses his sense of circumscribed identity. In his sense of oneness with Mediterranean nature and culture, he seems to find himself no longer in reality but rather thrust into what he calls "the play of appearances." Certainly one of the most striking descriptive passages in *The Wrong Side and the Right Side* occurs when the narrator attempts to explain his love of life as "a silent passion for what might perhaps escape my grasp, bitterness under a flame" (*EE 106*). Perhaps the single most beautiful section of the volume as a whole is the narrator's struggle to express the extreme fragility of the illusory world of appearances that mirrors his love:

> I was lucid and smiling as I faced this unique play
> of appearances. It seemed to me that a single gesture
> could have cracked this crystal in which smiled the

face of the world. Something was going to undo itself, the flight of the pigeons would expire and each bird would fall slowly on its spread wings. Only my silence and my immobility rendered plausible what so strongly resembled an illusion.... The world endured, chaste, ironical and discreet (like certain sweet and restrained forms of feminine friendship). An equilibrium established itself, colored nevertheless by the apprehension of its own end (*EE 105–06*).

In passages such as this, Camus demonstrates not only his Romantic sensibility to the union of the individual consciousness with the exterior world, but also his talent as a prose stylist. Beginning with his earliest writings, Camus conceived of literary creation as a response to the world of appearances, a response that required the elaboration of subtle and flexible forms of expression.

5. "L'Envers et l'endroit"
("The Wrong Side and the Right Side")

The final story of the volume, which has the same title as the collection as a whole, consists of a very short anecdote followed by reflections that pertain not just to that anecdote, but to all the other stories as well. "The Wrong Side and the Right Side" does not present us so much with new material as it consolidates what the author has already written.

In the introductory vignette, the narrator tells us of a woman who, having received a modest inheritance toward the end of her life, decides to supervise the construction of her own tomb. Each Sunday she visits it, and becomes so enamored of her future resting-place that all else in her life fades into the background. She takes such care of her tomb and its environs that the other visitors in the cemetery assume she is dead and begin to leave flowers in her "memory." The point of the vignette, of course, is that the woman, in preparing herself for death, has ceased living. Her cautious waiting-for-death has brought on a premature demise. Her actions represent, for the narrator, the *absurdity* of human endeavor (*EE 118*).

In the second, philosophical or moralizing section of the story, the narrator describes himself sitting at his desk on a January afternoon, observing the shadows on the window-curtains, "the play of the foliage and of the light" (*EE 116*) that shines through the curtains from the exterior world. This domain of beautiful appearances (described in more detail in "Love of Life") is what the narrator calls "l'envers du monde" (literally: the "wrong side of the world," but perhaps more accurately, the "other" side of things, their hidden essence, their often obscured but fundamentally real beauty). The play of light that comes from the "wrong" or "other" side is in diametrical opposition to the absurdity of human action, which, because it is both visible and constant, is called "l'endroit" or the "right side." Thus when the narrator pleads, "Until later the other things, men and the tombs they buy. But let me cut this minute from the cloth of time" (*EE 116–17*), we understand that although he recognizes the necessity of living with and among other people, of sharing their burdens, he also needs those moments of solitude and contemplation that lie "between yes and no" and that seem to hold the promise of an aesthetic or artistic meaning.

In the conclusion of the story we read: "One man contemplates and another digs his tomb: how can we separate them? Men and their absurdity?.... I am attached to the world by all my actions, to men by all my pity and my gratitude. Between this right side and this wrong side of the world, I do not wish to choose" (*EE 118*). In the end, therefore, as in each individual story, Camus the artist strives for a balancing of opposites, for a synthesis of apparent contrary forces. His desire not to choose one rather than the other—yes rather than no, Prague rather than Vicenza, the right side rather than the wrong side—indicates his willingness to live in a state of suspension between the demands of social and political reality on the one hand, and the inner impulse to contemplate the world of illusory appearances from which art springs on the other. Camus could not have known in 1937 that the synthesis of which he dreamed as a young man would prove increasingly difficult to achieve, both because of the monstrous developments of European history that were beginning to take shape, and because of his own dogged pursuit of technical mastery that allowed for no compromise, no half-measures, thus rendering the ideal of a final totalizing synthesis more distant with each succeeding work. For the moment, however, at age twenty-four, Camus had created a first noteworthy volume whose aesthetic unity and stylistic care seemed to foretell further and more ambitious textual experiments.

II. *Nuptials*

One year after the publication of *The Wrong Side and the Right Side* appeared a second slender volume entitled *Nuptials*. Once again, Camus's thoughts centered on the question of Mediterranean culture, and specifically, on the relative importance of individual human action and historical determination. Mediterranean civilizations exhibit a multi-layered archaeological record of the flourishing and dying of peoples; to examine the vestiges of the Roman, Byzantine, and Arab monuments left behind on Algerian soil is to contemplate the leveling power of Time, which reduces the grand designs of conquerors to fragments of broken stone. At the same time, the individual who visits these ruins necessarily wonders what place he might occupy in the large scheme of things, whether his projects and dreams will be subject to the same leveling force as that which has fractured the columns of temples and overturned triumphal arches. The essays of *Nuptials* pose the interrelated problems of culture, history, individual action and creativity, belief (whether religious in the traditional sense or pantheistic), and sensual immediacy (the situatedness of the self in the present moment). The volume is composed of four essays of unequal literary value, each of which I shall describe briefly, but only two of which I shall comment on in some detail.

The first two essays, "Noces à Tipasa" ("Nuptials at Tipasa") and "Le vent à Djémila" ("The Wind at Djemila"), are crucial both for an understanding of Camus's artistic sensibility and as examples of his early prose style. The last two articles, "L'été à Alger" ("Summer in Algiers") and "Le désert" ("The Desert"), are also of interest to the Camus scholar, but both betray evidence of their author's relative inexperience as a writer and exhibit a certain youthful self-satisfaction and easy virtuosity that will disappear in later years as Camus progressively eliminates directly revealed personal experience from his writings.

In "Summer in Algiers" Camus traces an idealized portrait of his native city. Writing directly in the first person, Camus is alternately serious and humorous about the qualities and shortcomings of his countrymen, whom he depicts as living for the pleasures of the moment, without any need for the transcendence or consolations of religion, without significant intellectual aspirations. Although Algiers is thus a city without virtue (in the traditional sense of that word), it nevertheless possesses its own idiosyncratic moral code, which Camus describes with sympathy and wit. At the end of his account, Camus includes an anecdote to illustrate this curious code in the street language of Algiers, called *Cagayous*. Throughout the essay, Camus identifies strongly with the Algerian working-class, with its hardships, but also with its capacity to enjoy the sensual pleasures of life to the fullest. There is, however, a certain cruelty to the headstrong pursuit of pleasure: one uses up one's energies at a very young age, then remains as a mere spectator in the wings while the next young generation follows the same hedonistic path. Despite the lightness of tone that characterizes the majority of "Summer in Algiers," the reader notes, as he did in *The Wrong Side and the Right Side,* Camus's empathy for the aged and for those facing imminent death in solitude. In a strikingly cryptic formula, Camus calls Algeria "ce pays où tout est donné pour être retiré" ("this country where everything is given only to be taken away") (*N*

42). The search for momentary satisfaction has a bittersweet edge: the gifts of life are tokens to be collected at the opposite shore.

In "The Desert" Camus continues his reflections on the tenuous balancing of life in its immediacy and the threatening horizon of death. But in this essay, the only one of the group that does not take place in North Africa, the tone is formal, even academic: none of the playfulness of "Summer in Algiers" is to be found here. Based on the second trip Camus made to Italy, in September 1937, and dedicated to his admired teacher and mentor, Jean Grenier, "The Desert" is a rather elaborate intellectual exercise whose message is somewhat obscured by the author's inflated rhetorical style. This essay is one of the very few examples in Camus's writings of verbal expression overshooting its mark, perhaps the result of the pupil's strong unconscious wish to impress his professor and guide. The central point of "The Desert" is clear, however: while visiting a cloister in Florence and while reading the evidence of resignation to inevitable death expressed on funereal inscriptions, Camus feels within himself an overwhelming revulsion. He refuses to accept either this attitude of resignation or the pale consoling phrases that accompany and justify it. For Camus, there is only life in the present moment, not in the hereafter, and his refusal to look beyond the world in its phenomenal appearance takes on the form of revolt (*révolte*). As we shall see in Chapter Five of this book, the notion of revolt is central to Camus's philosophical writings, and it is significant that the term is to be found at such an early stage of the writer's career.

Like Prague and Vicenza, Florence is the site of a

revelation: the city seems to offer Camus a privileged view of the essence of things. Here he learns the necessity of adopting what he calls a "double consciousness" that will accommodate both the "desire of duration" (the human being's wish to endure on the earth) and the "destiny of death" (our foreknowledge of the finitude of our actions) (*N 65*). It is this double consciousness that allows the author, in the concluding paragraph of "The Desert," to speak of the "fraternité secrète qui m'unissait au monde" ("the secret brotherhood that united me with the world") (*N 70*). The world becomes a vast temple *deserted* by the gods (hence the title of the essay) in which the individual, having chosen revolt as his mode of being, turns away from all religious and cultural forms of consolation, ready now to unite with the earth in its undisguised, merely sensuous form. In "The Desert" Camus expresses with some awkwardness the ideal of union between the human individual and the natural world, and attempts to bring together the notions of revolt and assent (*consentement*) in a higher synthesis: he wishes to demonstrate that within the very mood of revolt against the travesties of culture and religion lies a profound assent to the pure appearance of the geographical reality in which we live. Whereas "The Desert" only adumbrates this idea, "Nuptials at Tipasa" and "The Wind at Djemila" develop it at some length, with precision and clarity.

1. "Nuptials at Tipasa"

Between 1935 and the summer of 1937, Camus on several occasions visited Tipasa, the site of excavated

Roman ruins located some sixty kilometers from Algiers and in the vicinity of the Chenoua mountain. Tipasa is notable for the extensiveness of its monuments, which include a theater (for dramatic presentations and cultural events), an amphitheater (for sports), and a forum (the market-place and center of political debate), all in reasonably good condition. At the same time, the location of the ruins among luxuriant vegetation and at the foot of the mountain added an aesthetic dimension to their historical significance.

From the very beginning of the essay, Camus emphasizes the interpenetration of past and present, of legendary antiquity and current sensation. In the first sentences, we read:

> In the spring, Tipasa is inhabited by the gods and the gods speak in the sun and in the odor of wormwood, the ocean armored in silver, the sky of creamy blue, the ruins covered with flowers and the light rippling in the mass of stone. At certain moments, the countryside turns black from the sun. One's eyes attempt in vain to discern anything beyond drops of light and colors that tremble at the tip of one's lashes (*N 11*).

What Camus suggests here in powerful but controlled imagery is that the individual human being lives in a world suffused with the "voices" of the past: the ruins of Tipasa are not mere objective archaeological evidence, but they were and are the sacred enclosure housing the "speech" of the gods, which is still audible today if one lends an attentive ear. The gods address us not only through the stones of their temples, but also through the natural surroundings that have gradually overtaken and in some cases hidden these ancient fragments. It is the harmonious, melted or interwoven unity of nature and culture that interests Camus here. Chief among the natural elements is the sun, which blackens the fields and blinds the observer to the truth of his environment. Although at this point in the essay Camus seems to be describing in objective or literal terms the perspiration that clouds his vision, we should not underestimate the symbolic potential of the sun or of the theme of blindness as such. As we shall see in analyzing *The Stranger,* it is the blinding force of the sun that appears to incite Meursault to action and "cause" his crime; it is when the beach turns black from the sun's rays that the protagonist loses his bearings and stumbles, blindly, into murder.

In "Nuptials at Tipasa" the temporary loss of vision of the first-person narrator serves as a preliminary warning against an individual's temptation to think that he can fully comprehend both the natural and cultural contexts in which he lives. The gods (in the plural) to whom Camus refers are doubtless those of Greece and Rome; and a principal lesson of the myths of these civilizations is that the place of the individual human within Time and within historical evolution is small, perhaps even insignificant. On the other hand, however, engaged in the process of natural and cultural developments, one can attain a certain level of insight and dignity, and even tragic stature: the example of Oedipus comes to mind, the king whom Fate both trampled and elevated, granting him insight after blindness. I deliberately underline the Greek and Roman tonality of the essay because it seems to me that

Camus's attempts to "accorder ma respiration aux soupirs tumultueux du monde" ("harmonize my breathing with the tumultuous sighs of the world") (*N 13*) involve a tension based on a difference of scale: what the author desires is a merging with the earth, "nuptials" with Tipasa as natural *and* cultural site, yet can his own breathing be heard against the background of the *tumultuous* sighs of the world?

"Nuptials at Tipasa," despite the care with which Camus establishes the limits of the individual's realm of effective action, remains overall a lyrical expression of affirmation. Camus stresses especially what one can gain from embracing the truths that lie dormant in the stones and immediately accessible in the flowers and the sea; he espouses what he calls a "measureless love" (*N 16*) of the earth. In the terms of ancient philosophical tradition, Camus aligns himself with the Epicureans, who sought pleasure and assigned primary importance to the sensual realm. When he writes sentences such as "There is no shame in being happy" and "At Tipasa, I see is equivalent to I believe, and I do not persist in denying [rejecting] what my hand can touch and my lips caress" (*N 18*), we understand the central importance of sensual immediacy in this essay, the degree to which Camus rejects the dualism of mind and body in his unequivocal affirmation of the primacy of the physical as such.

2. "The Wind at Djemila"

In the spring of 1936 Camus visited the ruins of Djemila, a colony founded by the Roman emperor Trajan. One of his acquaintances, Marie Viton (a distinguished aristocrat of Protestant background who painted and who was to become a designer for Camus's Théâtre du Travail), was an amateur pilot; she flew the two hundred mile distance from Algiers to Djemila with Camus for a one-day excursion among the remains of Roman and Byzantine monuments.

As one might expect, some of the themes of the essay "The Wind at Djemila" echo the thoughts Camus had developed in "Nuptials at Tipasa." Once again, the relation of the individual to his natural environment is a central issue, and a reflection on the succession of conquering and colonizing powers that passed through the Algerian landscape only to disappear provides the author with an opportunity to discuss the lessons of history and of temporal mutability. As in the previous essay, the title contains an organizing metaphor: just as the notion of "nuptials" subtended much of what Camus said in "Tipasa," here the image of the "wind" lends a poetic quality to the author's introspection.

As was the case in "Tipasa," when Camus arrives at the site of the ruins, he encounters resistance: at Tipasa, that resistance was expressed by the narrating subject's "blindness"; here, it takes the form of the wind that buffets him, causing him to lose his sense of orientation and of the limits between his body and the world. At the beginning of "Djemila," Camus describes the merging of an individual consciousness and nature, whereby the human subject is reduced to the level of the plants and stones that surround him:

Like a pebble polished by the tides, I was glazed by the wind, worn to the soul. I was a part of this force in which I was floating, then completely submerged,

46

then I became the force itself, mingling the throb-
bing of my blood and the great sonorous beats of that
heart which is everywhere present in nature. The
wind was fashioning me in the image of the ardent
nudity that surrounded me (*N 25*).

Once he has joined completely with the wind and
with the "heart beats" of nature, once he has *become*
the force that transforms the physical world, Camus
has reached the level of pure presence: no longer do
thoughts of the future, of material well-being, of professional accomplishment, enter his mind. And, most
importantly, no longer does the issue of life after death
assume any relevance: the promises of religion have
no place in a world that has been reduced to the naked-
ness of the *now*. As the essay progresses, the author
makes increasingly clear his position on the side of the
ancient Greeks and against Christian dogma: he admires the former for their acceptance of the transitory
beauty and finitude of human existence, and refuses
what he considers to be the false consolations imagined
by Christians to "conceal from themselves the certainty of death" (*N 29*). As he states in a striking formula near the conclusion of the essay, "I wish to carry
my lucidity to its limit and contemplate the end of my
days with all the profusion of my jealousy and my horror" (*N 30*). From statements such as these, it is easy
to understand why Camus was so often the target of
the priests and preachers, who would inevitably characterize the author's attitude as one of pride and arrogance. Before condemning Camus, however, we should
not forget that his refusal of religion was also an act
of courage: to imagine nothingness after a life lived

and examined to its limit and to accept the endpoint of existence as a closed door is to place the highest *value* on the here and now, to refuse the deferral of justice and freedom until some later, transcendent but invisible and unverifiable Judgment.

In the final paragraph of "Djemila," as he observes the pigeons hovering around the broken columns of temples whose gods are no longer worshipped, as he meditates on the transitory quality of ambition, conquest, and triumph, Camus concludes: "In the end, the world always conquers history" (*N 32*). This is an appropriate conclusion for *Nuptials* as a whole as well as a crucial foreshadowing of Camus's later philosophical essays, notably *The Rebel*. Although always left-of-center politically, Camus ultimately had to reject the tenets of dogmatic Marxism because he could not believe in History as the end and justification of human action. Unlike Christians, Camus refused to look beyond the pure presence of the world, but unlike the Communists with whose ideology he only briefly engaged, he could not see in the evolution of historically determined factors alone a raison d'être for the life of the individual human. What Camus attempts to delineate as "Mediterranean values" in both *The Wrong Side and the Right Side* and *Nuptials* will never disappear from his work; his search for a balance between assent and revolt, creative solitude and political/social solidarity, history and the pure presence of the world will accompany him throughout his career.

CHAPTER THREE

L'Etranger (The Stranger) and

Le Mythe de Sisyphe (The Myth of Sisyphus)

I. The Stranger

Written for the most part in 1939 and 1940 in Algeria and published by Editions Gallimard in Paris in 1942, *The Stranger* was the first work by Camus to achieve notoriety in French intellectual circles. In the February 1943 issue of the influential review *Cahiers du Sud* Camus's novel was reviewed favorably both by his mentor Jean Grenier and by the existential philosopher Jean-Paul Sartre. Grenier emphasized the role played by the Algerian geographical and cultural context in the overall design of the text, and Sartre recognized both the structural clarity of the narrative and the moralizing impulse of the author, whom he compared in passing to Voltaire, the creator of *Candide* and of numerous other philosophically grounded satirical and allegorical tales. Because *The Stranger* appeared during the middle of World War II, when paper was rationed and publishing houses had to contend with Nazi censorship, its arrival on the Parisian literary scene did not guarantee its wide diffusion through a broad segment of the reading public. *The Stranger* enjoyed what the French call a *succès d'estime*—the approbation of a numerically limited but cultivated audience that could discern the revolutionary qualities of Camus's prose and of his moral vision.

Viewed as a whole, Camus's career, like that of most other artists, is not a linear progression of gradual steps leading smoothly from one achieved work to the next. Rather, it proceeds in a series of jumps and of hesitations, as the author continually shifts his attention from one literary form to another. Nevertheless, perhaps because he was more aware than many writers of the dangers of formal experimentation, Camus tried, from the very beginning, to structure his works in groups, each of which centered on one major theme. Thus, in the present instance, *The Stranger* was conceived to be part of a triptych that also included *The Myth of Sisyphus* and *Caligula*. All three texts have as their central concern the problem of the absurd (*l'absurde*), the meaning of which we shall encounter throughout the next two chapters. Crucial to an understanding of Camus's art is the combination of unity and diversity involved in this method of creation: on the one hand, because the three works all develop the notion of the absurd, Camus can point, justifiably, to a unifying thematic thread; on the other hand, since *The Stranger* is a novel, *The Myth of Sisyphus* is a philosophical essay, and *Caligula* is a play, there is also diversity of literary form. We know from Camus's *Carnets* (*Notebooks*) the extent to which he planned his writings far in advance, and most often according to groups or "cycles." As we begin to read *The Stranger*, we move into the cycle of the absurd.

If we ask the inevitable questions—what has changed since *The Wrong Side and the Right Side* and *Nuptials*? Why is *The Stranger* a work of incomparably greater value than its lyrical but aesthetically limited predecessors?—the answer lies partially in Camus's discovery of a prose style appropriate to his theme, and partially in the universality of the conditions and experiences his novel depicts. In his review of *The Stranger*, Sartre had noted the strong affinity between the extremely simple, sometimes colloquial discourse used by the first-person narrator and what the French had come to call the "American style"—that of Ernest Hemingway in particular, who, reacting against the European tradition of the "psychological novel," tended to eliminate the meanderings of subjective consciousness from his protagonists in favor of a straightforward (or apparently straightforward) presentation of the world in its flat outward appearance. Hemingway's characters seem merely to tell us what they see and do not invite us to descend into their innermost selves. The same could be said of the hero of *The Stranger*, Meursault, who appears to live at the surface of things, to ask few questions of himself or of others, to show a remarkable indifference toward his surroundings and his own threatening fate.

Although the early readers of *The Stranger* found in its pages stylistic innovations of a distinctly modern mode, at the same time they detected resonances from a much older tradition—namely, Greek myth. Camus's novel may be one volume of three devoted to the analysis of existence in its twentieth-century absurdity, but it is also a prose drama conceived and developed along the lines of antique tragedy. It is this blending of the very new and the very old that makes of *The Stranger* a text as compelling in the 1990s as it was in the 1940s. Indeed, one might say that the text's rootedness in myth has assured its survival beyond the necessarily limited duration of the "American" style and of the phase of existentialist humanism in which the theory of the absurd temporarily attracted its adherents. When I used the word "fate" in the previous paragraph, it was in the sense of Greek tragedy: Meursault is driven to commit his crime by a force that seems to reside outside himself, outside his conscious will. It is the enigma of the crime—why it took place, why the protagonist's actions tended inexorably toward this catastrophe—that resides at the very center of the novel.

1. Plot and Structure

The Stranger is divided into two nearly equal parts. In the first of these, Meursault (who is the main character as well as the narrator) tells us of events in his life leading up to his apparently unpremeditated or "unconscious" murder of an Arab on a beach near Algiers; in the second large segment, he describes his detention in prison and his trial in chronological sequence, from the moment of his arrest to the final hours before he faces the guillotine. In the first section of the book, therefore, we witness Meursault's life as a free man—a bachelor less interested in his modest employment than in the simple pleasures of his activities outside of the office. It should be noted that Camus places Meursault in the same kind of working-class neighborhood in which he himself grew up, and that the pleasures his character describes—those of swimming and sunbathing, sensuality in its various forms—are those that Camus had described in his early essay "Summer in Algiers," noting that such moments of

52

enjoyment, being free of charge, are available to everyone, regardless of social standing. When Meursault is imprisoned, he does not regret material comforts that he did not have in the first place, but merely the freedom to do something *or* nothing, in the location of his choice.

From a first reading of the narrative in its broadest contours, one can see that Camus is interested in analyzing the problems of guilt and of judgment: under what circumstances does a human being become guilty in the eyes of society, and in what precise ways does society, through its legal system, presume to deprive that individual of his freedom?

The trial scenes in Part II of the novel constitute the culmination of the plot. In order to convince the jury that the crime on the beach was not the product of blind chance but the logical result of Meursault's "criminal mind," the prosecuting attorney must have access not only to the events of the day in which the alleged murder was committed, but also to the activities of the protagonist in previous days and weeks. The prosecution wishes to establish the indelible character traits of a man who, on a given day, was capable of murder. In a curious way, the reader of *The Stranger* finds himself in the same position as the prosecuting attorney—in possession of numerous facts and clues that, taken together, combine to form a portrait of Meursault. Yet the burden of our reading is to determine whether or not the protagonist can be considered guilty; in considering the *same* clues as the prosecution, how is it that we can arrive at a different conclusion? Or, stated in reverse, how is it possible for an attorney to twist or distort events to such a degree that an innocent man becomes guilty? Before engaging in these interpretive difficulties, we must now examine the novel's plot and structure in more detail. Following is a schematic overview:

PART ONE

Chapter One: Meursault receives a telegram with the news that his mother, who had been living outside of Algiers in a nursing-home, has died. He obtains permission to take time away from work to attend the funeral, which is preceded by an all-night wake. During the wake he is disturbed by the brightness of the lights that are kept on throughout the night in the chalk-white room in which his mother has been laid to rest; he also has the disagreeable impression that the mourners at the nursing-home are sitting in judgment of him. The funeral takes place under the blinding sun.

Chapter Two: Having returned to Algiers, Meursault spends his Sunday relaxing. While swimming he runs into Marie Cardona, who attracts him physically. They go to a film starring Fernandel (a French actor who appeared in many comedies and who was famous for his outrageous facial "mugging"), then return to Meursault's apartment for the night.

Chapter Three: A man named Raymond Sintès, who lives on the same landing as Meursault, comes to visit. He asks Meursault to write a letter for him. We learn that Raymond circulates in the Algerian underworld and is a pimp. He has fought recently with the brother of a woman he has been keeping; he suspects the woman of being unfaithful to him and decides to send her an insulting letter, which will be penned by the protagonist.

Chapter Four: Marie asks Meursault if he loves her: he finds her question meaningless and does not reply unequivocally. Raymond quarels violently with the woman to whom he sent the insulting letter, and receives a warning from the police. Without judging Raymond's actions, Meursault finds that the former has been kind to him and accepts his friendship. Another neighbor of Meursault, named Salamano, loses the dog he was accustomed to insulting and beating every day and is disconsolate in his loss; this event causes Meursault to think of his mother.

Chapter Five: Meursault is not enthusiastic when his boss offers him the opportunity of a promotion and a position in Paris. He seems indifferent when Marie asks him to marry her. Raymond invites him to the beach on Sunday.

Chapter Six: Located exactly at the center of the novel, this chapter sets the scene for the crime, which Meursault commits in its concluding pages. Raymond and Meursault take the bus to the beach and are followed by Arabs, whom Raymond suspects to be the brother of the woman he has insulted and some of his friends. At the beach, they spend time at a cottage owned by a certain Masson and his wife. After a swim, a copious lunch, and several walks along the beach, Meursault kills one of the Arabs. At the time, he is blinded by the rays of the sun.

PART TWO

Chapter One: Meursault is henceforth confined to prison. He talks to the examining magistrate, who wishes to uncover the motives of the protagonist's crime and who declares his own belief in Jesus Christ. The magistrate assures Meursault that Christ can "save" him.

Chapter Two: In this chapter, Meursault describes the routine of prison life and the transition he undergoes as he begins to think no longer like a free man, but like a prisoner. While evoking the ways in which he seeks to avoid boredom, he mentions a newspaper article he discovers under his mattress. The article contains the account of a man in Czechoslovakia who returns home after many years' absence and decides to surprise his mother and sister by not at first revealing his identity when he takes lodging at their small hotel. The mother and sister kill him for his money, then discover his real identity. This anecdote will be the basis for *Le Malentendu* (*The Misunderstanding*), a play Camus wrote in 1944.

Chapters Three and Four: Camus presents the trial of Meursault in these two chapters. Throughout the trial, the protagonist finds that the matter of his crime is being treated as an abstract event completely separate from his person; in listening to the attorneys present their arguments, he has the uncanny feeling that they are relating someone else's story. Most crucially, it seems to Meursault that he is being condemned not so much for having killed a man as for *not* having cried at the funeral of his mother. His attitude of fundamental "indifference" dominates his character-study as formulated by the prosecution. At the end of the trial, when asked why he killed the Arab, Meursault answers: "because of the sun" (*E 158*). This response evinces laughter in the courtroom.

Chapter Five: In this final chapter of the novel, the reader is closest to the protagonist's inner thoughts, which include an interesting reflection on capital punishment as well as a meditation on the meaninglessness of life. Like the Camus of *Nuptials,* Meursault refuses the consolations of religion and concludes that one must learn to live without hope in an absurd world. As the dawn of his execution approaches, Meursault looks back on the simple pleasures of his existence, remembers his mother, opens himself to "the tender indifference of the world" (*E 186*), and hopes that a large crowd will greet his death with cries of hate.

Viewed as a structural whole, *The Stranger* is organized around three deaths: that of Meursault's mother in I,1; that of the Arab in I,6; and the imminent death of Meursault himself in II,5. Five chapters separate each death from the next; Camus very consciously achieved a perfect symmetry in the form he gave to his novel. In calling attention, structurally, to the theme of death, the author naturally challenges the reader to formulate an interpretation that can take into account each of its occurrences: one major role of the reader is to discover the unity that underlies each scenic or dramatic presentation of this essential organizing motif. In the next section of the current chapter, I shall approach this interpretive problem in some detail, but without presuming to exhaust its significant potential.

2. Interpretation

Until at least twenty years after its initial publication, a strong critical consensus existed on the overall

57

significance of *The Stranger*. It was assumed that Camus had created, in the figure of Meursault, a modern Everyman—a person possessing neither outstanding virtue nor vice, living at the surface of an existence for which there could be no transcendental justification. Although the protagonist does not possess qualities in the traditional sense (he is not ambitious in his job and shies away from commitment in his relationship with Marie), neither is he someone whom one would suspect of setting out, consciously, to harm another human being. In most early interpretations of the novel, both critics and non-specialized readers concurred that the protagonist was, at bottom, a sympathetic character, and that the vagaries of circumstance (his chance presence on the beach at a given moment) were to blame for his unpremeditated act of violence against the unknown Arab. According to this view, Part II of the novel is essentially a satire and an indictment of the French judicial system, which must assume the responsibility of condemning to death a man whose guilt is highly problematic. Such a reading of the text also concurs with the thoughts and judgments of Meursault in the final chapter (II,5), when he elaborates his theory of the absurdity of human existence. The notion of the absurd as developed in *The Stranger* depends upon a confrontational relation between the misunderstood and mistreated individual and a society whose rules and laws hover in an abstract realm beyond his control and comprehension. In this sense, early readers of *The Stranger* were tempted to find parallels between the universe of Camus's first novel and that of Franz Kafka, whose faceless heroes wander through the endless alienating maze of inhuman and distant bureaucracies.

The kind of interpretation I have sketched here rests on the reader's sympathy for the protagonist and on his willingness not to judge Meursault as harshly as the prosecuting attorney. In other words, such an interpretation depends on the reader suspending his own judgment, on his refusing to *become* a judge in the act of reading. The question that arises inevitably, however, is the following: is it advisable or even possible for the reader of a complex and challenging literary text to suspend his judgment in this way? Could it be that by doing so he neglects to notice some of the text's most important but least visible threads? Before moving to an examination of the imagery and symbolism of *The Stranger,* I would like to focus briefly on the matter of Meursault's character and on the problem of moral responsibility that seems to call for the reader's full engagement in an act of judgment.

Although it is difficult to accept the prosecuting attorney's portrait of Meursault as a man possessing a "criminal mind," nevertheless some reference or recourse to the protagonist's past activities and to the milieu in which he lived may not be without significance. That is, the people with whom Meursault chooses to spend his time are important to our understanding of him as an individual. Principal among these, of course, is Raymond. The fact that the protagonist does not disdain to greet him or to accompany him to the beach may not be of great interest, but the fact that he wrote a letter for his neighbor, a letter whose content is not morally admirable, *is* significant. In this

59

particular context, Meursault's so-called "passivity" (he accepts writing the letter "to satisfy Raymond because I had no reason not to satisfy him"—*E 54*) calls for interpretation: although he may have had no cause to refuse assistance to a neighbor, certainly the content of that assistance is not irrelevant in the moral sphere. Further, if one examines closely the development of the plot, it becomes clear that the sending of the letter sets in motion the essential action of the novel. It is because of the letter that Raymond has a quarrel with the woman he keeps, gets in trouble with the police, and finally is followed by the Arabs; and it is because the Arabs are on the beach at a specific time that Meursault commits his crime. Meursault's passivity and indifference, his refusal to judge Raymond's behavior, make of him the latter's silent accomplice or even, one is tempted to say, puppet. If this is the case (if this interpretation is plausible), it becomes difficult to sympathize with the protagonist and difficult to take at face value his theory of the world's absurdity. A reader willing to adopt a moral stance might say that the real absurdity in the novel resides in Meursault's blind association with Raymond, a man whose way of living and whose values should be easy enough to decipher (and to refuse).

It may be that Camus, like many novelists, dispersed his own personality through the text of *The Stranger,* dividing himself, so to speak, among various characters. In traditional interpretations of the novel, Camus "is" Meursault. But, interestingly, in deciding to give Raymond the last name of *Sintès,* his own mother's maiden name, Camus may be presenting the darker side of himself in indirect, fictive form. In this case, one possible reading of the book would show the fundamentally innocent Meursault being manipulated and driven to crime by his guilty alter ego. If the text supports such a reading, one cannot easily dispense with moral issues or with the twin questions of judgment and responsibility.

What I am suggesting here is that there is no one canonical interpretation of *The Stranger* because of the ambiguities inherent in its mode of presentation. It may seem, on a first reading, that Camus has loaded the dice in favor of his protagonist, that Meursault is essentially the plaything of Fate and the victim of an injust judicial system. At the same time, however, the troubling friendship between Meursault and Raymond Sintès (on a couple of occasions, Raymond asks the hero to be his *copain*—his "buddy" or "pal") might cause the reader to question in a fundamental way the apparently simple or innocent demeanor of a man who has, after all, killed a fellow human. This kind of ambiguity emerges perhaps most visibly on the moral level I have evoked, but also comes to the surface in the imagery of the novel, in the highly coherent and continuous symbolism that inhabits the text. In the final section of my discussion of *The Stranger,* I would like to turn to the three death scenes and to their symbolic potential.

3. "Because of the Sun"

All readers of *The Stranger* will remember the striking formula pronounced by the inculpated protagonist when asked, in the moments preceding his definitive imprisonment, why he committed his crime: "because of the sun" (*E II,4,158*). To the curious spectators at the trial, this phrase is worthy only of derisive laughter, in that it seems to beg the question of the intent or possible culpability of the accused. To the reader of the preceding sections of the novel, however, the phrase makes sense, not only because of the preeminent role played by the sun in the death scene on the beach, but also because of its presence throughout the text as constantly returning leitmotif.

The image of the sun and of light in general is the principal organizing factor of I,1, the opening chapter in which Meursault attends the wake and funeral of his mother. It is noteworthy that the night of the wake is never described in nocturnal terms, but always with emphasis on the blinding light that suffuses the whitewashed room in which Meursault and his mother's former companions are gathered together. When, in this context, the protagonist says that he is "blinded by the sudden splash of light" (*E 17*) that covers the small room's naked walls, he foreshadows not only the sky's "unbearable burst of light" (*E 28*) on the next afternoon, at the moment of the burial, but also the sun's "unbearable burst of light on the ocean" (*E 85*) at the dramatic moment immediately preceding his killing of the Arab. The sun and the light seem to have a numbing effect on Meursault; their unbearable (in French, *insoutenable*) force causes him to lose all conscious control of his actions. In I,1 this emotional numbness translates as the apparent indifference of the protagonist toward his mother's death—a lack of expressivity that the prosecuting attorney will equate with callousness. In I,6, however, the sun will blind

Meursault to such a degree that he *acts* in a way that transforms his life.

The second death scene, in which Meursault kills the Arab, is not just "at the center of the novel," it *is* the center of the novel. The way in which one reads this particular scene will determine one's overall reading of *The Stranger*. Here, the solar imagery attains its greatest intensity, but the sun is not the only significant element in the mythical-symbolic framework of the chapter. It would seem that Camus constructed the center of his novel on a complex interplay of masculine and feminine elements, both on the level of the human participants in the drama and also on the level of Nature as mythic or tragic repository of superhuman power.

We must remember, first, that Raymond and Meursault choose the beach on the outskirts of Algiers as a place of repose but also as a refuge: they are successfully followed, however, so that the calm of their haven from the troubles of the city proves to be fragile. The threat to Raymond and to Meursault comes from the male world of the Arabs' planned revenge. Throughout the chapter, Meursault is in a somnolent state. After swimming with Marie, he falls asleep; and after lunch his wanderings on the beach are those of a sleepwalker. Most curious and most interesting in the structure of the chapter is the fact that *three* walks are taken; in the first, Raymond is wounded; in the second, the Arabs disappear before Raymond can provoke them and cause a second fight; and in the third, Meursault walks alone until he encounters the one Arab he will kill. After the second walk, there is no particular reason for the protagonist to continue along the beach, and his words of explanation for his not entering the cottage with Raymond are strange but most likely significant:

I accompanied him [Raymond] to the cottage and, while he was climbing the wooden stairway, I remained in front of the first step, my head ringing from the sun, discouraged at the effort I would have to make to climb the stairs and once again face the women. But the heat was such that I also found it painful to remain immobile under the blinding rain of the sun that fell from the sky. To stay here or to move on came to the same thing. After a moment, I returned to the beach and I began to walk (*E 91*).

The one phrase that seems especially curious in this all-important transitional moment concerns the "effort" involved in "facing" the women: neither Marie nor Masson's wife represents a threat to Meursault, especially when compared to the Arabs, who are still on the beach. Lest this detail seem merely gratuitous and insignificant, it appears again one page later at the crucial moment at which the protagonist discovers the Arab:

I could see from afar the small dark mass of rock surrounded by a blinding halo made of light and of sea spume. I thought of the cool source behind the rock. I wanted to find again (*retrouver*) the murmur of its water, I wanted to flee the sun, the effort and the women's cries (*les pleurs de femme*), I wanted, finally, to recapture (*retrouver*) the shadow and its repose. But when I got closer, I saw that Raymond's guy [i.e., his adversary and recent assailant] had returned (*E 92*).

In this poetically evocative passage, we encounter once again a detail curiously unmotivated in the immediate context of the scene—the "women's cries" which have no visible antecedent or point of reference. That Camus is not alluding to any specific cries or tears is clear in the French "les pleurs *de* femme"— cries typical of women in general rather than of any particular woman who inhabits this novel. It would seem, then, that avoidance of "women" in some very general sense is a major motivating factor in Meursault's walk, as well as avoidance of the sun. In French, *le soleil* (the sun) is masculine, and its attributes are those traditionally associated with masculinity. If we combine the level of the human participants with that of the natural symbolism that builds throughout the passage, we see that Meursault is fleeing both some vague and undefined female danger, and also the blinding rays of the sun, which are compared, at the end of the scene, to a "long shimmering blade" (*E 94*). At the same time, however, he longs to find again or to recapture the "cool source" and the "murmur of its water" that lie behind the rock—and therefore, beyond the present moment of his confrontation with the Arab. Avoidance of "the women" and of the sun combines with a regressive desire to *re*-capture a "source" that has been lost. Since *source* in French is feminine, and since it not only denotes origins but carries with it liquid connotations, it may be that indirectly and metaphorically the carefully described scenic presentation of the place in which murder will occur is also, simultaneously but on an unconscious level, an evocation of the place of birth, of the source of life. Hiding or veiling this most sought-after and

65

least attainable of sources is the adult world, a world of choices that Meursault has difficulty making: to write or not write an insulting letter, to be or not be Raymond's friend; to kill or not kill the Arab; to marry or not marry Marie Cardona. In fleeing the sun and "the women," in yearning for the source behind them, the protagonist aspires to a state of primordial innocence and tranquillity that is inaccessible in reality, yet permanently desirable. In this sense, an image of Meursault's mother is reintroduced into the text by poetic indirection before the mother is mentioned directly: indeed, two pages after this description the protagonist tells us that the blinding sun is "the same as on the day I buried Mother" (*E 94*).

It is not my purpose, given the limited scope of this book, to delineate a detailed and elaborate interpretation of *The Stranger* based on a psychological or Freudian model. My comments above have as their unique goal to suggest that the scene in which Meursault's mother appears directly—in death—is not the only one in which her presence impinges on the text and its symbolical significance. At the very end of the novel, when the protagonist gives us his theory of the absurdity of human existence, when his language has become argumentative, logical, and abstract, when all traces of myth or symbol seem to have disappeared from the text, we read:

> Noises from the countryside now reached me. The smells of the night, of the earth and of salt refreshed my brow. The marvelous peace of this summer entered me like the tides.... For the first time for a long time, I thought about Mother (*E 185*).

In the end, all three death scenes are inhabited or haunted by the pervasive image of the mother. The "tender indifference of the world" (*E 186*) toward which Meursault opens himself just before his own death reminds us necessarily of the tender indifference that existed between the young narrator of *The Wrong Side and the Right Side* and his mother, that silent shadowy presence we recognize as a transparent representation of Catherine Camus, née Sintès. What has changed between Camus's early series of stories and *The Stranger* is that the maternal image is no longer merely a direct and recognizable borrowing from reality, but has become a rich amalgam of fictional figuration and symbolic imagery. While Camus's first important novel is ostensibly about the absurdity of life, it is also a prolonged meditation on one man's expulsion from the source of his earliest protected existence, on his fall into the alienated and arid realm of the sun, in which his natural indifferent somnolence resists the harsh imperatives of individual responsibility and moral choice.

The Myth of Sisyphus

As we turn from *The Stranger* to *The Myth of Sisyphus,* we move from one aesthetic form to another, from a short novel to a philosophical essay. It will be remembered that Camus studied philosophy at the University of Algiers before he began his career as a journalist; although his health prevented him from becoming a professor in the state-run educational system, throughout his life he continued to read philosophical texts, both classical and contemporary. Yet only twice did Camus choose the philosophical mode of inquiry for the exposition of his own ideas, in 1942 for *The Myth of Sisyphus* and in 1951 for *The Rebel*. Both of these works are crucial to an understanding of Camus's thought and both are important in the evolution of the history of ideas in our century. At the same time, however, *The Myth* and *The Rebel* do not occupy as central a position in twentieth-century philosophy as *The Stranger* and *The Plague* in modern literature. The essential reason for this is that Camus, unlike Husserl or Heidegger or Sartre, did not organize his ideas within a rigorous conceptual or theoretical framework: he is not the inventor of a new *system* of philosophy. He writes in the French tradition of Montaigne and Pascal, in which systematic conceptualization is less important than psychological acuity, finesse of moral observation, and elegance of style. Thus, although in *The Myth* Camus alludes with great frequency to philosophers known for the density of their abstruse formulations, his own style is always clear and to the point. He states in the first pages of his treatise that his method will consist less of "learned and classical dialectics" than of "common sense and sympathy" (*MS 18*). As we read *The Myth of Sisyphus,* we need to keep in mind that Camus's essay is "philosophical" not in its language or essential form, but rather in its rootedness in the European philosophical tradition. In my own comments that follow, I shall emphasize the development of the essay—its logical and rhetorical organization—as well as the relevance of the thoughts it delineates to Camus's other works, especially his prose fiction.

1. General Organization of the Essay

The Myth consists of four sections of unequal length followed by an appendix. In the first section (entitled "Un Raisonnement absurde" or "An Absurd Argument"), Camus poses the problem of his essay—the question of whether or not suicide can be justified and whether or not the taking of one's own life is the logical solution or inevitable consequence of what he calls the *absurdity* of the human condition. Camus wishes to determine whether there is or can be a "logic unto death" ("logique jusqu'à la mort"—*MS 24*): can we live our lives in such a way that we do not fall into half-measures and compromise; is it possible for us to pursue our thoughts and our commitments to the very end of the exacting demands they place on our action? And if so, will this end-point be suicide or some other form of absolute engagement yet to be defined? The first sub-section of "An Absurd Argument" (called "L'Absurde et le suicide" or "The Absurd and Suicide") sets up these questions and leaves them provisionally open. In the next three sub-sections of "An Absurd Argument," ("Les Murs absurdes" or "Absurd Walls," "Le Suicide philosophique" or "Philosophical Suicide," and "La Liberté absurde" or "Absurd Freedom") Camus develops at some length what he means by *the absurd* and explains in what precise way his argument differs from the logic of those philosphers and thinkers he refers to as "existentialists." He concludes "An Absurd Argument" with a meditation on freedom and on the necessity of *revolt*—a term that is central to *The Myth* but also to *The Rebel*.

In the second large section of the essay, entitled

"L'Homme absurde," or "Absurd Man," Camus gives three examples of what he calls "absurd lives"—that is, lives pushed to the limit, in which the human being has done and attained all that can be reached within the bounds imposed by mortality. The three examples given—that of Don Juan and his amorous exploits, that of the dramatic actor (in French, the *comédien*), and that of the military conqueror—may strike the reader as unusual and idiosyncratic, but, as we shall see in a more detailed analysis later, each of these figures incorporates a variation on the theme of the *morale de la quantité* that Camus opposes (and prefers) to the limiting qualitative emphasis on moderation and self-control that characterizes traditional philosophical ethics (concretely: the exploits of Don Juan, the subversive masks of the actor, and the self-exalting conquests of Alexander, all represent the diametrical opposite of the Greek ideal of the "golden mean," according to which mastery of one's desires and domination of self constitute the worthiest goals of a life well-lived).

In the third section of the essay, entitled "La Création absurde," or "Absurd Creation," Camus addresses the relation of the work of art to the absurd. He asserts that the former should not be a "refuge" from the latter, but that any artistic creation worthy of the name should be, or attempt to be, "an absurd phenomenon" in its own right (*MS 131*). That is: the role of art is not to console us or to obfuscate from us the absurd nature of our condition as human beings, but rather to reveal that absurdity and to stand as an act of *revolt* against our condition. In this section, Camus includes interesting remarks on the points of

70

intersection between literature and philosophy, and warns against the temptation inherent in all works of art to "explicate" the world from a set philosophical or ideological perspective rather than manifest it in its lived complexity (*MS 136*). Also in this section is a discussion of some of Dostoevsky's characters and a critique of the Russian novelist's tendency to resolve their dilemmas, to reduce their confrontation with the absurd to a specific and definable existential situation. In this context, Camus makes use of the term "metaphysical reversal" ("renversement métaphysique") to describe the way in which Dostoevsky "chooses against" his fictional characters (*MS 151*): we shall discuss this notion in more detail later.

The fourth section is entitled "Le Mythe de Sisyphe," or "The Myth of Sisyphus." Camus has constructed his essay in such a way as to lead from the posing of a philosophical problem—that of the justification and significance of suicide—to the retrospective grounding of that problem in myth. The well-known myth of Sisyphus, taken from ancient Greek tradition and reinterpreted by Camus, will provide a useful and clear illustration of the problems with which the author dealt logically and argumentatively in the previous sections. Like most myths, that of Sisyphus exists in several mutually conflicting versions, which Camus rehearses at the beginning of the chapter. In each version, however, it would seem that Sisyphus (who, according to Homer, was at one time the wisest and most prudent of mortals—*MS 163*) in some way defied the power and the patience of the gods, and was punished in a particularly cruel way: he was condemned to roll an enormous rock up a steep slope, then

71

watch it roll down, only to begin the same task anew, forever. The labor of Sisyphus, unlike those of Hercules, accomplishes nothing; it has become the symbol for useless work undertaken in despair. In his reinterpretation of the myth, Camus makes of Sisyphus an "absurd hero," not only because the latter faces the absurdity of the human condition more concretely than any one of us, and in infinite repetition, but also because he is able, without indulging in "metaphysical reversals," to *comprehend* the essential meaning of his condition. Camus imagines that when Sisyphus arrives at the top of the slope, he reflects upon his fate and achieves self-consciousness:

> It is during this return, this pause that Sisyphus interests me. . . . This hour which is like a welcome breathing and which comes back as surely as his misfortune, this hour is that of consciousness. . . . Sisyphus, proletarian of the gods, impotent and rebellious, knows the extent of his miserable condition: it is on this condition that he reflects during his descent. The clairvoyance that was intended as his torment simultaneously serves his triumph. There is no fate that cannot be surmounted by scorn (*MS 165–66*).

Camus's reinterpretation of the Greek myth is thus a *reversal* of its traditional message. At the very end of the main body of his essay, Camus writes: "We must imagine Sisyphus happy" (*MS 168*). This "happiness" is not frivolous contentment, of course, but rather the deeper pleasure one attains in understanding one's fate and in achieving an intellectual mastery over the physical conditions that seemed at first to be all-encompassing and all-constraining. At the end of the fourth section, Camus states with the greatest decisiveness that suicide is *not* the necessary or logical end-point of an existence pushed to its extreme limits, but that the human being can learn to live with and within absurdity through an act of consciousness that gives him mastery over all situations, even those of apparent total despair.

In the definitive version of *The Myth of Sisyphus* is included a short Appendix entitled "L'Espoir et l'Absurde dans l'oeuvre de Franz Kafka," or "Hope and the Absurd in the Works of Franz Kafka." Camus originally intended for this section to be included within the body of the essay, but it could not be published in the original 1942 version because it dealt with the fictions of a celebrated Jewish author all of whose writings had been banned by the Nazis. When censorship had been lifted after the end of the War, Camus retrieved the Kafka chapter and had it placed immediately following the main part of the argument. As we shall see in a moment, the section on Kafka repeats much of what Camus says in his discussion of Dostoevsky, and constitutes a confirmation of the important distinction between the existential and the absurd that subtends the entirety of the essay's development.

2. Analysis of Key Terms

In my comments on the general organization of *The Myth of Sisyphus,* I have emphasized the structure of Camus's argument and several of the essay's central ideas. In doing so, the most I have hoped to accomplish is to provide the reader with a preliminary way of access to the complex issues raised by *The Myth*. As a next step, I would like to focus on several key terms in the essay—terms that have a definite meaning for Camus and the clear comprehension of which is a prerequisite for our understanding of *The Myth* as a whole.

a. The Absurd

A standard dictionary definition of the adjective "absurd" is "unreasonable" or "incongruous." Thus, if I speak of an "absurd world," I mean a world that does not seem to exhibit qualities or properties that correspond to my sense of reason: in looking at the world, I see incongruities rather than a structured or organized totality. Crucial to what I have said here is the subject—object duality within which I have formed my statement. I am not saying that, in an absolute sense, the world *is* absurd, but rather that it appears so to my consciousness, which is used to functioning within a framework of reason or reasonableness. Camus alludes to this framework when he gives his clearest definition of the absurd in the essay:

> I spoke too quickly when I said that the world is absurd. This world in itself is not reasonable, that is all one can say about it. But what is absurd is the confrontation of this irrational phenomenon with the passionate desire for clarity whose call resonates in the depths of man (*MS 39*).

In the first stages of *The Myth,* Camus establishes both the irrational nature of the world as he sees it and the desire for clarity that resides in the human being.

In stating categorically that the world is not "reasonable," Camus distances himself both from Christians (who find in their natural surroundings the traces of God's eternal presence) and from doctrinaire Marxists (who believe that the teleological movement of History guarantees the significance of each passing moment). According to the author of *The Myth,* the struggle of each individual against the unreasonableness of the world presupposes the total absence of hope, the constant refusal of all consolations, and conscious dissatisfaction with the human condition *in* its absurdity (*MS 51–52*). In stating his position in these absolute (and apparently, absolutely negative) terms, Camus begins to engage in a polemic against those thinkers whom he designates as "existentialists."

b. Existentialism and the Existentialists

Although the term "Existentialism" has a long and not uncomplicated history, it is often associated with the philosophy of Jean-Paul Sartre. Since Camus argues consistently against what he calls the "existentialist view" of the world in *The Myth,* one might assume that he is arguing, in a thinly veiled way, against Sartre. This is not the case. Although Sartre and Camus had differing philosophical and literary perspectives throughout their careers, they did not engage openly in polemical dialogue until the publication of *The Rebel,* which Sartre found dangerously naive in its lack of attention to the historical determination of human action (we shall return to the debate surrounding *The Rebel* in Chapter Five). In *The Myth,* Camus may have Sartre in mind on occasion, but he focuses

explicitly and at length on the Christian existentialists Kierkegaard and Chestov, and, more briefly, on
the phenomenologist Husserl.

Stated in the most general of terms, the existentialists, whether atheist or Christian, do not believe that
a transcendental "essence" pre-exists the human being: rather, they proceed from the assumption that one
must first study the *existence* of humans in their specificity before moving toward an examination of their
essential qualities. Thus the Danish philosopher Kierkegaard and his Russian commentator Chestov both
examine the contradictions and incongruities of the
world as well as the crises of faith within the individual before asserting God's presence and availability to
us. The first step—the laying-bare of incongruities—
resembles Camus's theory of the absurd; but the second step, in which the level of existence-within-the-
world is transcended by a "leap of faith," is made
neither by Camus the philosopher-essayist nor by the
heroes of his fictions. Whereas Kierkegaard uncovers
the absurdity of the human condition only in order to
assert that, in the end, one must believe *because* it is
absurd (that is: one believes in a superior Being who
holds the secrets of the phenomena that *seem* unreasonable to the limited human intelligence, but that
have a higher significance within the Divine Order),
Camus refuses this form of "consolation" and remains
within the confrontation that sets apart the individual
desirous of clarity from the irrational environment in
which he lives. Hence Camus's concise formulation:

> The theme of the irrational as conceived by the Exis-
> tentialists is that of human reason first losing itself

in confusion, but then finding deliverance in its own negation. The absurd, on the other hand, is lucid reason recognizing its limits (*MS 72*).

Throughout the first half of *The Myth,* Camus sets his own thoughts apart from those of the existentialists. For our purposes, the crucial point is the fundamental distinction Camus makes between his theory and the systems of the philosophers to whom he alludes. The fact that the author of *The Myth* discusses the difficult philosophy of the German phenomenologist Husserl in three pages, and the fact that Husserl is juxtaposed to Kierkegaard and Chestov, with whom he shares no real affinities and virtually no thematic material, is a matter for philosophers to ponder and, no doubt, to criticize. The rapid simplifications that characterize some passages in Camus's treatise will offend professional philosophers more than the readers of *The Stranger* and *The Plague,* who will find in *The Myth* ample theoretical justification for the author's fictional constructs.

c. "Morale de la quantité"

In the transitional passage that concludes the first long section of *The Myth* ("An Absurd Argument"), Camus explains the development of his argument in these terms: "Having begun with the anguished consciousness of the inhuman, the meditation on the absurd returns at the end of its itinerary to the very heart of the passionate flames of human revolt" (*MS 90*). If one does not accept the "consolations" imagined by the existentialists, therefore, but if one refuses to move beyond the world *in* its absurdity, then the only logical path of human action lies in revolt. As we have seen, the second major section of the essay, entitled "Absurd Man," gives three examples of "absurd lives"—lives pushed to the limit, in which human possibilities exhaust themselves. Camus chooses figures like Don Juan and Alexander the Great because they exemplify his *morale de la quantité:* their conquests, whether amorous or military, never find satisfaction. One triumph leads inevitably to another, and the only important victory is the one that lies ahead. Similarly, the actor, or *comédien,* is never pleased with just one role, but is a chameleon constantly changing masks. In preferring quantity to quality, exhausting conquest to moderate enjoyment or tranquillity, Camus proclaims the necessity of constant revolt in the face of irremediable absurdity.

d. Metaphysical Reversal ("Renversement métaphysique")

The two novelists often associated with the existential tradition who appear at length in *The Myth* and who in some ways influenced Camus's writings before and after the composition of the essay are Fyodor Dostoevsky and Franz Kafka. Camus admired Dostoevsky for having integrated into his novels a remarkable diversity of human types and temperaments, and especially for having posed the problems of suicide and of madness at a level perhaps not reached by any other writer. The author of *The Myth* sees in Dostoevsky's diaries and in his fictions "logic pursued unto death, exaltation, 'terrible' freedom, the glory of the Czars become human" (*MS 148*). Yet Camus also finds in the transition from *The Possessed* to *The Brothers Karamazov* a turn away from the absurd and toward the saving grace of God. He quotes one of the final pages in *The Brothers Karamazov,* in which Aliocha, one of the principal characters, when asked whether there will be life after death, responds: "Certainly we will see each other again, we will joyously tell each other all that has happened" (*MS 149*). This turn—from dwelling within the absurd to belief in a transcendental significance for all human experience—constitutes what Camus calls a *metaphysical reversal,* and makes of Dostoevsky an existential novelist rather than an absurd novelist (*MS 150*). Camus sees the same essential movement in the transition from *The Trial* to *The Castle* in Kafka's fictional universe. Whereas the wanderings of the protagonist in *The Trial* seemed endless and groundless, Camus sees in certain pages of *The Castle* the manifestation of a divine guidance and of an all-embracing metaphysical significance. In examining both Dostoevsky's and Kafka's literary works, Camus expresses admiration for the universality of their artistic vision; but he distinguishes between universality and truth, and himself prefers to tell the "truth"—i.e., the undisguised story of the world's unconquerable absurdity (*MS 185*).

3. The Uses of Myth

In the end, perhaps the greatest strength of Camus's essay is its intelligent and resourceful use of ancient mythology to express a modern philosophical position. What the author writes in the early pages of his treatise about the absurd, about the insufficiencies of the existentialists, about the *morale de la quantité,* and about metaphysical reversal, gains final clarity and resolution in his reinterpretation of the Sisyphus legend. It is Camus's ability as a writer to place himself within the traditions of Greek thought but to restructure that thought for his own purposes that lends his essay a power of persuasion that it would have lacked without reference to the myth. As we begin to read the works that follow *The Stranger* and *The Myth of Sisyphus* chronologically, we will note Camus's increasing reliance on mythical symbolism and on ancient literary tradition. This reliance is never a sign of intellectual dependency, but rather an indication of the writer's talent in organizing his thoughts and thematic material around a central core that, in its very mythical structure, possesses meaning for a wide variety of readers. Although Camus's best works certainly contain individualized and particularized features—in setting, character, and atmosphere—they distinguish themselves from less successful writings by their general or universal appeal. Camus criticized Dostoevsky and Kafka for choosing universality over "the truth." But if we read Camus today, it is not because what he says about the absurd, for example, is "true" within the confines of a particular philosophical debate in the mid-twentieth century, but rather because his thoughts *in* their expressive form bear the stamp of their carefully reworked, artistically transmuted origins.

CHAPTER FOUR

Caligula
and
La Peste (*The Plague*)

I. *Caligula*

The first Paris performance of *Caligula* took place on September 26, 1945, with Gérard Philipe in the title role. Camus had worked on this his best play for a number of years (notes on the principal themes of *Caligula* can be found in the author's *Carnets* (*Notebooks*) very shortly after the completion of *Nuptials* and at the earliest stages of the composition of *The Stranger*), and was to revise it on a continual basis until 1958, when it achieved its definitive form. As we shall see, *Caligula* is a play based on ideas that are central to Camus's general philosophy or world-view; its dialogues echo both the problem of the absurd as developed in *The Stranger* and *The Myth of Sisyphus* and also the theme of revolt as found in *The Plague* and *The Rebel*.

Although the Parisian audiences of 1945 were unanimous in their praise of the acting talent of Gérard Philipe (who was to become one of France's greatest luminaries in the theater and in the cinema), the first reviewers of *Caligula* expressed reservations about the play's sometimes verbose and extravagant scenes, in which the expression of intellectually complex views seemed to take precedence over dramatic action and the continuity of the plot line. Like Sartre, Camus had created a "theater of ideas": he placed characters on the stage with whom, for the most part, the spectator would have difficulty identifying and empathizing, but whose profound moral and spiritual dilemmas would constitute an enigma worthy of one's concentrated attention. The principal purpose of the theater according to Camus was to make the audience think, to shock it into reflection by upsetting its mental habits and routines. In choosing one of the most puzzling and outrageous figures from ancient history as the central character of his drama, Camus could guarantee his spectator both an intellectual challenge and an aesthetically enhanced questioning of the values on which cultivated human beings have traditionally based their laws, their arts, their civilization as such.

Caius Caesar Germanicus (12–41 A.D.), surnamed Caligula because, as a young man living in a military camp in the Roman province of Germania, he wore soldiers' sandals (called *caliga* in Latin), began his reign as Emperor in an enlightened, liberal style, but soon underwent a complete change in his personality. Historians traditionally have assumed that an illness of some sort was responsible for the transformation of Caligula into one of Rome's worst tyrants, into a man who forced his subjects to adore him as king and as a god. Influenced by his Egyptian slaves, he worshipped the goddess Isis, and himself demanded to be recognized as "The New Sun." His four-year reign was characterized by arbitary arrests and murders; he himself was assassinated in 41 A.D.

1. General Content and Structure of the Play

At its most basic level, *Caligula* is a study of excess—excess of desire, of power, and even, as we shall see, of idealism. As was the case in *The Myth of Sisyphus,* there is no place in the universe of this play for moderation or tranquillity of spirit. Like Don Juan, the metamorphosing *comédien,* and the military conqueror, who led exemplary "absurd lives" in *The Myth,* Caligula pushes his own existence to the limit of its possibilities. At the same time, however—and it is herein that the imaginary worlds of *The Myth* and of *Caligula* do not coincide—in his play Camus is not content to present the problem of the absurd from the perspective of the individual consciousness: as spectators, we are not merely aware of the Emperor's aspirations, volition, despair, and crimes, but also of the way in which his actions impinge upon the lives of his subjects and advisors. Nowhere in *The Myth* does Camus consider the consequences of Don Juan's seductions or Alexander's triumphs; the people who fall victim to the grand designs of the "absurd heroes" remain invisible to the philosopher-essayist. This is not the case in *Caligula,* where Camus was careful to surround his Emperor with secondary characters who must choose between passive fear of the tyrant and open resistance to his schemes.

The entirety of the play is constructed on a balancing of the Emperor's actions against the reactions of the characters with whom he comes into daily contact. Camus has his audience penetrate the claustrophobic world of a ruler's inner sanctum, in which court intrigue (what, in today's jargon, we would call "political in-fighting") is rampant and transparent. As spectators, our gaze is always directed at Caligula, but occasionally we must view his thoughts and actions through the interposed consciousness of the courtiers.

The play begins with the clear and direct exposition of the problem: why and in what way has Caligula changed? During the first two scenes of Act I we do not see the protagonist, but hear about him from his concerned courtiers, who worry at his inexplicable absence. The general assumption is that the Emperor has left the palace out of grief for his sister Drusilla, who has died just recently. It had been rumored for some time that brother and sister had an incestuous relationship, but this possible "fact" does not seem to account for Caligula's recent behavior and for the brusqueness of his departure. When we encounter Caligula for the first time, we see a man who is distraught and disheveled, who is suffering from an inner crisis at first difficult to define. In the first important prolonged scene of the play (I,4) he tells us of his desire to possess the moon, and states, in a bland tone: "Les hommes meurent et ils ne sont pas heureux" ("Men die and are not happy") (CA 27). It is the coupling of the Emperor's strange, apparently mad aspirations (expressed initially as his desire to "have" the moon) with his discovery of the absurdity of human existence (our unhappiness *and* our mortality) that sets in motion the various dramatic conflicts of the play.

In Act I, after an expository section on Caligula's past and on his current unstable frame of mind (scenes 1–7), we witness the changed ruler's first decree, which foreshadows all the atrocities to come. Caligula orders all citizens of the Empire to disinherit their children and to will their fortunes to the State (I,8). In so doing, the ruler wishes to "change the order of things" and to "confound the categories" on which civilized society is based (*CA 40*). He now sees his function not as law-giver and guarantor of civil peace, but rather as all-powerful judge in need of guilty persons for the exercise of his arbitrary power. The first act ends with Caligula contemplating himself in a mirror.

There is an interval of three years between Act I and the three remaining Acts of the play. Camus has chosen to show us the very beginning of Caligula's transformation and the bloody conclusion of his reign, and has kept close to historical chronology. At the beginning of Act II, we learn, once again through the eyes of the courtiers, not only what the Emperor has done in concrete terms, but also the rumors circulating about him: we learn that the populace at large lives in fear of his every act, all the more so since there seems to be no reasonable explanation for his choices and decisions. In Act II we meet the two most important secondary characters in the play, both of whom serve as foils to Caligula: the first, Cherea, a man of common sense who desires nothing more than an undisturbed existence; the second, Scipio, a poet whom the Emperor simultaneously admires and mocks. At this point in the play, we observe what might be called Caligula's "distorted logic." He liberates the slaves in his palace so that senators might serve him (II,5), and he declares that everyone in his realm must ultimately die *because* he is absolute master (II,9). In other words, everyone is by definition a slave and everyone is by definition guilty in an Empire that knows only arbitrary whim and decree.

Act III begins with a grotesque scene: we witness Caligula disguised as "Venus" emerging from behind a backdrop of his own making. In this short instance of "play within a play," we discover how important theatricality has become to the Emperor. He desires to be the protagonist in a drama of his own creation; his spectators, of course, are not allowed *not* to applaud. Adding to the outrageousness of the scene itself (the actor who plays Caligula wears a woman's tunic, makes effeminate gestures, and at one point paints his toenails) is the blasphemous arrogance of the ruler: he informs his subjects that it is through his power that the gods are able to descend to earth (III,1). Caligula is not merely portraying Venus in an outlandish way: he is suggesting that he participates as much, or perhaps more, in godliness, than she. When Scipio observes that Caligula's actions are indeed blasphemous, the latter responds: "No, Scipio, it's dramatic art. The error of most men is not to believe sufficiently in the theater. Otherwise they would know that it is permissible for anyone to stage celestial comedies and to become god. One need only harden one's heart" (*CA 97*). As Act III progresses, Caligula demonstrates the extremes to which he is willing to carry his arbitrariness. When he discovers incontrovertible proof that Cherea is among a group of conspirators seeking to depose him, the Emperor decides, on a whim, to destroy the proof and thus to declare Cherea "innocent." In so doing, Caligula acts not out of uncharacteristic altruism, but rather in defiance of all logic (and even his own self-preservation) so that he might surpass even the gods in his power. In his dialogue with Cherea, Caligula puts it this way: "with the disappearance of this proof I see the dawn of innocence on your face. What an admirably pure forehead you have, Cherea. Innocence is so beautiful! Admire my power. The gods themselves cannot restore innocence without prior punishment" (*CA 112–13*).

As could be imagined, Act IV is, in the strict Greek sense, the *catastrophe* of the play—that is, the final action in the drama that negates or overturns all that has preceded. The conspiracy that Caligula chose to ignore for his own reasons of power and of narcissistic self-absorption succeeds in the end. The Emperor cannot stand in the way of an inevitable death that he himself has caused: the suffering that he has inflicted on the people surrounding him returns in his direction in a final moment of retribution. Caligula, by the conclusion of the play, has refused the tranquil happiness sought after by Cherea, the love offered him by his mistress Caesonia, and the promise of fulfillment in art as achieved by the poet Scipio. He has affirmed that the only real happiness consists of "universal disdain, blood, hate all around me, the unequaled isolation of the man who holds his entire life in his vision, the measureless joy [*joie démesurée*] of the unpunished assassin" (*CA 148*). In the end, of course, it is precisely this thirst for the limitless, the *démesuré,* that causes the protagonist's downfall, that brings on his ultimate and tragic punishment.

2. Interpretive Issues

a. Excess (Démesure)

At the end of the first section of *The Myth of Sisyphus* Camus had asked the question: "Is there a logic unto death?" (*MS 24*). The purpose of the remainder of the essay was to prove that such a logic did indeed exist, but that its end-point, rather than being suicide, was the lucid acceptance of the absurdity of the world coupled with an obstinate, constantly renewed revolt of the consciousness. The hero of *The Myth* is the individual human who knows himself to be condemned to a universe characterized by the irrational but whose desire for clarity is never assuaged. Although at first there might seem to be very few points of contact between the noble mythical figure of Sisyphus and the ostensibly "unhinged" Caligula, nevertheless it is notable that the point of departure of Camus's play is exactly the same as that of the philosophical essay. At two crucial points of *Caligula,* the protagonist asserts his will to "remain logical until the end" (*CA 26; 105*). The first instance of this phrase is near the beginning of the play (I,4), when Caligula notes, on the one hand, that all people are unhappy and destined to die, and, on the other, that he wants to possess the moon. In this context, to be logical until the end means to deny one's own mortality (to become a god) and to pursue an object that is properly inaccessible. The second occurrence of the phrase is in a monologue that Caligula pronounces in the scene preceding his important confrontation with Cherea (III,5). At this stage of the play, the protagonist is surrounded by the death and destruction that he himself has caused, and realizes that even if he could possess the moon now, this "transfiguration" of the world would not reverse the course of events nor would it restore life to those who had disappeared through the arbitrariness of his decrees (*CA 105*).

The dialogue between Caligula and Cherea in III,6 is one of the pivotal moments in the play, in that for the first time Camus clearly opposes to the protagonist's philosophy of excess another philosophy, another way of being in the world. This is one of the brief and rare moments in the dramatic progression in which the spectator manages to look beyond the bloody realm of the Emperor, to glimpse a far calmer horizon. In response to Caligula's exposition of his thirst for absolutes, Cherea says:

> I want to live and to be happy. I think that neither is possible when one pushes the absurd to its limit. I am like everyone. To free myself from my condition, sometimes I wish for the death of those I love, I desire women whom the laws of family and of friendship prohibit me from desiring. To be logical, I should then kill or possess. But I judge that these vague ideas are not important. If everyone tried to realize them, we could neither live nor be happy (*CA 109*).

The principal difference between Caligula and Cherea is that the latter, in accepting the limitations of his human condition, refuses to follow the logic of his desires to their conclusion. Cherea's notion of happiness is one of moderation and simplicty; according to him, the realization of one's wishes is not equivalent to a life well-lived. Within the universe of *Caligula,* Cherea's statements are noteworthy for their extreme brevity and for their disappearance under the sheer weight of the protagonist's will-to-power. Yet we should remember what Cherea says and the simplicity with which he speaks, because his mode of reasoning and his conception of life foreshadow the stubborn modesty of Dr. Rieux, the hero of *The Plague*.

b. Power, Evil, Resistance

In reading *Caligula,* we must not forget that the play was written during World War II and performed not long after the Liberation. The 1930s and first part of the 1940s in Europe had been a period in which political democracy had been under siege, both from the Nazi far-right and from the Marxist far-left. Following a world-wide economic depression came a total war that submerged the Continent in death and in despair and that caused dislocation to all political systems that advocated the freedom of the individual. The first audiences of Camus's play were not insensitive to the fact that the Roman Emperor, in his abuse of power and in the arbitrariness of his decisions, could be likened to much more recent despots—Franco, Hitler, Mussolini, and Stalin come to mind—all of whom had followed a certain "logic" to its most extreme political and social consequences. Camus's play did not deal in mere abstractions, therefore; the problems of power and of evil had emerged as being historically real, incorporated as they were in the concrete manifestations of bombs, torture chambers, and death camps. In *Caligula* the spectator experiences the inevitability with which the pursuit of an absolute degenerates into the exploitation and enslavement of human beings, who have become mere means to the end of the dictator's narcissistic enjoyment of his short-lived capacity to alter the face and facts of the world.

In his representation of the Emperor's entourage,

Camus has given us an interesting portrait of fear and courage as well. Most of the secondary figures in the play live in awe of Caligula's power and fawn on him at every opportunity, much to his distaste (abject flattery is boring to an intelligent if devious monarch). But two of the characters—Cherea and Scipio—stand up to him, and both gain the respect of their adversary. In these courageous individuals who are unwilling to succumb to the will and vision of their ruler, post-war French audiences could see fictional/theatrical equivalents of those of their countrymen who had joined the Resistance. What I am suggesting here is not that *Caligula* be reduced to a mere political allegory (this was certainly not the author's intention), but that we recognize in its form of representation the potential for direct political and historical relevance. Put differently, one might say that the era in which *Caligula* no longer resonates with such relevance will be a happy one indeed: a time when dictators no longer exist and have become incomprehensible because they are unimaginable.

c. Judgment and Art

Throughout the play, when Caligula exercises his formidable power over his subjects, he most often assumes the role of judge. The Emperor, precisely because he has absolute political authority, presumes to be both judge and jury; no voice of opposition can be heard in his realm, which is also his universal court. Toward the middle of Act IV, when his actions have reached the epitome of arbitrariness, Caligula orders the organization of a poetic contest, in which he will evaluate all entries (IV, 12). The contestants are given one minute to write a poem on the subject of death. We learn in this scene that Caligula himself has penned a treatise on the same theme, and that the lyrical but excessively subtle literary efforts of the court poets apparently fall short of the insights the ruler thinks he has gained on death during his three years of tyranny. At the conclusion of IV,12 Caligula sends away the poets (perhaps an allusion to Plato's famous banishing of the poets from his Republic) and chooses to keep only Scipio, whose verses seem to have moved him. In a very important short assertion, Caligula reveals to us why he considers himself to be an artist and why he feels justified in condemning the writers of mere ornamental verse: "I have written only one composition. But in it I prove that I am the only artist Rome has ever known, the only one, you know, Cherea, who has made his thoughts and actions coincide" (*CA 137*). What Caligula implies here is that his reign can be "read" as one enormous "poem": his monstrous acts, in his view, amount to artistic creation. The only reason he spares Scipio from his generalized condemnation of the court art-functionaries is that he finds in Scipio a temperament or sensibility somehow attuned to his own. He cannot judge an individual who has, in his own way, understood death.

At the end of the play, the two characters who remain untouched by the increasing folly of the Emperor are Cherea and Scipio—those two individuals in whom Caligula sees strong resistance to his power and whom he is, therefore, incapable of judging. In a crucial sense, the entirety of *Caligula* turns on the question of judgment. In his final monologue, as he contemplates himself one last time in the mirror before succumbing to the conspirators, the protagonist raises the question of his guilt, and cries out: "But who would dare condemn me in this world without a judge, in which no one is innocent?" (*CA 149*). If we move back to the beginning of the play, we can see that Caligula's initial discovery of the absurdity of the world (the unhappiness and mortality of the human being) caused him to assume that the very notion of innocence was an impossibility. We are all condemned to death and to subsisting for a while on a planet characterized by the irrational. Given the absence of innocence, there can be no judges, *unless* one presumes to become the unique judge and redefine the parameters of innocence and guilt. Caligula's reign of terror begins and ends when he decides, in an act of egocentric will, to *create* (by constantly disrupting and redefining them) the lines of demarcation between guilt and innocence.

Caligula the arbitrary judge is thus at the same time Caligula the artist of evil. The unusual combination of the themes of judgment and of art is at the center of the play; the way in which we interpret the subtle interplay of the two apparently disparate elements will determine our overall reading of *Caligula*. Further, although the overwhelming atmosphere of evil and of excess is perhaps unique to this one play, nevertheless we can see echoes of its thematic network in other works of Camus. The problem of judgment per se is, of course, the organizing principle of *The Stranger* (which poses the question of the possibility of innocence in an absurd world in a different register from that of *Caligula*); but it also reappears in *The Fall*, where the protagonist, a lapsed member of the

93

legal profession, weaves a devious web of theatrical confession in order to implicate his listener/reader in his own guilt. Jean-Baptiste Clamence, the anti-hero of *The Fall,* is in some ways the negative image of Caligula: rather than use absolute power to achieve his objectives, he creates, artistically, an abject persona whose lucid recognition of his own human frailty becomes a lure to trap us in hopelessness.

As we move now to *The Plague,* the work that brought Camus international recognition as one of the major writers of the twentieth century, a novel characterized by a sober, almost neutral style, we should keep in mind, as a literary foil, the theatrical *démesure* of *Caligula.* In his play, Camus represents Evil as that which cannot be contained, as a form of violence that can only be undone by more violence; in his famous novel, as we shall see, a different picture emerges, in which the struggle against irrational forces establishes its claim to dignity.

II. *The Plague*

Written for the most part during World War II, *The Plague* did not appear until June 1947, when paper restrictions had been lifted and when the reading public had begun, once again, to buy books. The Gallimard publishing house, for which Camus now worked on a regular basis as reader and editor, anticipated correctly that the new novel would be successful, and ordered a first printing of 22,000 copies—a large number for a serious work by a man whose name, though well-known in intellectual circles, was by no means a household word. Four months later, to the surprise of even the most sanguine members of Gallimard's editorial board, *The Plague* had sold 100,000 copies; it was, by anyone's standards, a best-seller. Although literary fashion is fickle, *The Plague* has continued to be read regularly by successive generations, and forty years after its initial publication it had sold nearly three million copies in France alone.

As was the case with *The Stranger,* Camus's second novel owed at least some of its appeal to its use of mythical or symbolical elements. In fact, the use of the symbolic mode is so coherent and so continuous in *The Plague* that we might best use the term "allegory" to describe its essential literary form. On the simplest and most evident level, the novel tells the story of the violent outbreak of the plague in Oran, one of Algeria's major ports and industrial centers. (Camus had worked here as a journalist, so that his descriptions of the city and its inhabitants had a ring of authenticity.) But from the moment of the novel's publication, readers suspected that the plague might be the indirect representation or transposition of some other "disease" that returns periodically, like an epidemic, to interrupt human routine and bring with it death and destruction: in 1947, the universal consensus was that the plague stood for war, and specifically, the horrors of World War II. As we shall see, this reading is fully justified (Camus inserted numerous hints in the text that tend to set up an equation between the disease and the act of war), as long as we do not limit the novel's significance to a merely transparent and univocal allegory. The significant potential of the plague encompasses war, but includes other levels of meaning as well.

Before beginning the actual composition of his novel, Camus had read various chronicles from ancient and more recent history on important outbreaks of the plague and had consulted medical texts as well on the symptoms of the disease. Readers of his book will find that the plague appears in all its literal physical horror, and that the allegorical process did nothing to mitigate its realistic representation. Camus had read not only Daniel Defoe's *A Journal of the Plague Year* before beginning his own novel, but also, and most crucially, Herman Melville's classic *Moby-Dick,* in which Captain Ahab's obsessive search for the great white whale involves not only symbolism (the whale as emblem of absolute evil), but also long passages of a realistic nature describing life aboard a large armed fishing-vessel. Similarly, Camus chose to depict the plague first as a real epidemic with recognizable features, and second as a symbol of a malevolent force whose effects transcend the physical realm.

1. Plot, Structure, Characters

Like *The Stranger, The Plague* has a coherent progressive plot and an overall structural design exhibiting balance and symmetry. The novel is divided into five large sections, each of which contains numerous short chapters. In Part One (*P 9–68*), the narrator (whose identity remains undetermined until the end of the book) describes the city of Oran, introduces all the major characters, and relates the first stages of the outbreak of the plague. Part One concludes with the official declaration of the epidemic; Part Two (*P 71–165*) begins with the closing of the city's gates. In this second section, as the plague becomes more pervasive, the narrator focuses successively on the main characters in order to illuminate the precise individual ways in which they decide to confront the phenomenon of the disruptive disease. In some cases, members of the city's populace adopt a defeatist perspective, assuming that no amount of human effort can stem the tide of the epidemic. In other instances, individuals decide to pool their efforts and to face the plague in a "common front." In his clear contrast between the defeatists and the participants in the unified struggle, Camus is doubtless juxtaposing, via allegorical transposition, the Collaborationists to the members of the French Resistance during World War II. In the various conversations and confrontations that take place in Part Two, Camus establishes the importance of moral choice and of consequent action in the face of the epidemic. Part Three (*P 169–86*), located at the exact center of the novel, is the shortest of the sections. At this point, the plague has superseded all other concerns, all other issues in Oran. The narrator tells us that henceforth his story will not concern individuals so much as the collectivity. The universe of the novel now is engulfed in death; the citizens of Oran live only for the moment, without memory and without hope (*P 183*).

In Part Four (*P 189–263*), Camus brings together the essential narrative threads and moves his novel toward its dramatic apex. One of the city's doctors invents a serum and tries it out, first without success; but gradually it appears to gain effectiveness, and the section ends on a note of hope. The narrator deepens his analysis of the relationships among the characters, especially the friendship that has developed between

Dr. Rieux, the protagonist, and Jean Tarrou, a courageous and somewhat enigmatic man whose philosophy of moral action occupies one of the central scenes in the section. Part Four also includes a very important passage on religion that echoes some ideas that had been expressed in less elaborate form in Part Two. In Part Five (*P 267–309*), the epidemic lessens in intensity, then dies out. The doors of the city reopen, and the citizens of Oran, who had lived a long exile, now are reunited with their families. For Rieux, however, the "Liberation" from the plague occurs, ironically, just after the death of his friend Tarrou and after he has received news of his wife's death (she had left the city before the outbreak of the disease, and Rieux had had to live with virtually no news of her during her absence). At the end of the novel, as the citizens of Oran begin to resume their habitual existence, Rieux reveals that he has been the narrator. He tells us that despite the strong evidence of human frailty (cowardice, "collaboration," compromise of all kinds) that emerged during the period of the plague, nevertheless he can assert: "there are in people more things to be admired than to be despised" (*P 308*).

The overall structure of *The Plague* resembles that of a French tragedy in the classical, seventeenth-century tradition. Like the plays of Racine and Corneille, Camus's novel is divided into five "acts" (parts or sections), each of which has its own specific function. Part One, like the first act of all classical dramas, is essentially an exposition—an introduction of the principal characters and a first intimation of the work's central themes. In Part Two, the themes begin to be developed and the relations among the characters become more complex (sub-plots begin to emerge). Part Three, like the third act of many classical plays, is quite short and serves as a point of convergence for the themes, which, in intersecting with each other, produce a high degree of conflict. It is at this juncture in the work that all hope seems to be lost, and that a tragic outcome assumes an ominous inevitability. In Part Four, the work attains its greatest intensity, and the dramatic conflict that had been prepared in the previous section now erupts; characters with whom the reader had gradually empathized now succumb to despair and death. In Part Five, the tragedy deepens, but at the same time a resolution is reached: the protagonist, and with him the reader, gains insight into the meaning of the events that have transpired. The death and the hopelessness of the previous four sections are by no means forgotten, but the protagonist, like the tragic hero, has reached a higher level of awareness of his environment and of his life.

The Plague is Camus's longest prose fiction and, along with *The Rebel,* is his most ambitious work. Unlike *The Stranger* or *The Fall,* which center uniquely on one character, *The Plague* can be described as the imaginary recreation of an entire community. The self-effacing narration of Dr. Rieux emphasizes not his own thoughts or anguish, but rather the actions and reactions of Oran's populace as a whole. Thus, the narrator does not speak in his own name until the very end of the novel, and alternates between the use of the pronoun "we" and the expression "our citizens" in order to express his solidarity with people whose suffering has deprived them not only of hope but even of individuality. The plague is a leveling force that robs its victims of personal identity; as the deaths multiply, each individual human becomes increasingly faceless.

Despite his lucid realization of this leveling effect, however, the narrator finds in his immediate surroundings several fellow citizens who, because of the strength of their convictions or the compelling influence of their personalities, emerge as full-fledged characters in his chronicle. Most important among these are:

1. Tarrou: a man of independent means who has come to Oran after having had a very active, adventurous life. He becomes Rieux's best friend and indefatigable associate during the time of the plague. He is an astute observer of human nature and keeps a diary which the narrator occasionally cites to corroborate or to complete his own account.

2. Paneloux: an intelligent and socially committed Jesuit priest known for the persuasive power of his rhetoric, in both written and oral form. He delivers two important sermons, one in Part Two, the other in Part Four, both of which express views contrary to those of Dr. Rieux (and of Camus, whom Rieux "represents" rather transparently in these passages). He has great difficulty finding a suitable religious justification for the suffering brought on by the plague, but he is no coward and dies courageously soon after delivering the second sermon.

3. Rambert: a journalist from Paris who, having come to Algeria to undertake investigative reporting on the living conditions of the Arab poor, finds himself trapped in Oran because of the plague and separated from the woman he loves. Although he tries at first to escape from Oran illegally, eventually he joins the Sanitary Teams organized by Tarrou.

4. Grand: an unassuming civil servant who, at the beginning of the novel, helps save a neighbor named Cottard after the latter has attempted suicide. Grand is a would-be writer who struggles endlessly (one might almost say, in a Sisyphian manner) with one descriptive sentence in order to achieve stylistic perfection. In some ways, he appears ridiculous, but as the plague progresses, Grand turns out to be one of the strongest members of the Sanitary Teams, for which he does administrative work in his after-hours. Rieux sees in the modest Grand the most appropriate "hero" for plague times.

5. Cottard: a man who is sought by the police and who, at the beginning of the novel, unsuccessfully attempts suicide. He is the happiest of all Oran's citizens during the time of the plague because throughout this period the police have higher priorities to attend to than his arrest. He lives only for himself, never joins to help those suffering around him, but often confides in Tarrou, who finds him to be an interesting psychological "case." After the end of the plague, Cottard once again becomes mentally unbalanced (he fires a gun from his window into the street, where the newly liberated Oranese are dancing), and is arrested.

6. Othon: a local judge who at first distances himself from the "Sanitary" (i.e., Resistance) movement, but joins finally at the end of Part Four, after the death of his young son. The tragic and, in Rieux's (Camus's) eyes, unjustified death of this boy is at the center of the philosophical disagreement between Rieux and Paneloux.

7. Rieux's mother: although she does not play a major role in the novel, her silent but loving presence

reminds one necessarily of Camus's own mother and of her fictional appearance in *The Wrong Side and the Right Side*. (It is perhaps significant that the only two female characters in *The Plague* are Rieux's wife and his mother, and that they are remarkable in their near-invisibility. The world of *The Plague* is decidedly a man's world.)

8. Dr. Rieux: the protagonist and narrator of the story. He is a very devoted doctor, a careful observer of the people and events around him, and a scrupulous friend. He does not believe in grand actions, but finds "certainty in the work of every day" (*P 46*), in the dogged struggle of which each individual is capable according to his own talents. At the end of the novel, he has lost both his wife and his friend Tarrou; at the same time, however, he has become a more fully integrated member of the community in which he lives, and has discovered the meaning of human solidarity.

2. Interpretive Issues

Like *Caligula, The Plague* can be read as the representation of absolute evil and of the efforts made by certain individuals to struggle against its power. Whereas in *Caligula* only Cherea and Scipio had the courage to face the tyrant and to force him (if only briefly) to consider the magnitude of his misdeads, in *The Plague* a group of people band together and learn the value of common action. What separates Camus's novel from his play is the new emphasis placed on the theme of community or solidarity. Like the Enlightenment philosopher Jean-Jacques Rousseau, who theorized in *The Social Contract* that the welfare of the public at large was not the magnified mirror-image of each individual's happiness, but rather the product of the sacrifices and renunciations every person must make toward the difficult achievement of a common good, Albert Camus realized that the fight to contain and neutralize the plagues that have overcome twentieth-century civilization necessitates the surrender of egocentric goals and self-satisfied tranquillity. At the same time, however, Camus recognized and respected the inevitability of each human being's desire for personal happiness. The key interpretive issues of *The Plague* center in the delicate balancing of the personal and the public spheres; each of the novel's main characters attempts to find his own solution to the moral dilemmas that emerge from the conflict of these separate but equally compelling realms.

a. "Abstraction" and the Happiness of the Individual

During the first stages of the epidemic, the populace of Oran does not wish to recognize the reality of its new predicament. As increasingly large numbers of rats die in the streets and as more and more of the city's citizens fill the hospitals, it should be evident to everyone that "normal life" is no longer possible. Those who resist this realization cling to a desire for security and initially refuse to grasp the fundamental necessity for solidarity in the face of the all-encompassing crisis. This is the case for the journalist Rambert, who, on temporary assignment from Paris, declares to Rieux: "But I am not from here!" (*P 89*). To say that he is not *from* Oran means that the events *in* Oran do not concern him. In the important conversation between Rambert and Rieux that ensues, the former holds on desperately and blindly to his need for personal happiness, while anticipating, despite himself, the need for common action against the ravages of the plague. In attempting to counter the impeccable but unpleasant logic of the protagonist, Rambert asserts: "I know you are about to speak of public service. But the common good is composed of the happiness of each person" (*P 90*). As the novel progresses, Rambert learns that there is happiness, or at least fulfillment, in public service, and that a merely private happiness based on pleasure and contentment cannot be justified under the particular conditions created by the plague. In this sense, Rambert's political/social stance evolves from opposition to Rousseau's theories to an acceptance of their premises.

In the early period of his resistance to the reality of the epidemic, Rambert accuses Rieux of living "in abstraction" (*P 91*). That is: the journalist implies that the essentially unfathomable disease with its mysterious origins is more important to the doctor than human happiness in its concreteness. Rieux's response to Rambert does not occur audibly in the conversation, but is available to the reader in the narrator's transcription of his inner reflections: "Yes, there was in misfortune no small part of abstraction and unreality. But when the abstraction begins to kill you, it becomes necessary to trouble yourself with the abstraction" (*P Ibid.*). At the end of the passage, Rieux's conclusion on this issue foreshadows the primacy of common or group action that will characterize the novel as a whole. The doctor, aided by his diverse associates, will continue "the monotonous struggle between the happiness of each person and the abstractions of the plague, which constituted the entire life of our city during this long period" (*P 94*).

In the specific context of Camus's second novel and its central allegorical significance, the "abstraction" to which the narrator refers is doubtless that of war (and war, in 1947, meant World War II). Yet Camus uses this term elsewhere in his nonfictional and directly political writings, in order to express the unenviable position of humankind in the post-war age of ideological struggle and nuclear armament. In one of his most important essays on the perilous situation of the immediate post-war era written in 1948 and entitled "Ni Victimes Ni Bourreaux" ("Neither Victims Nor Executioners"), Camus declares that we live in a world of "terror" in which persuasion, rational discussion, and dialogue in general are no longer possible. He explains in these terms:

we live in a world of abstraction, that of offices and machines, of absolute ideas and of Messianism without subtlety. We suffocate among people who think they have a monopoly on truth, whether through their machines or ideas. And for all those who can live only in dialogue and in friendship with their fellow humans, this silence is the end of the world (*V 119*).

Readers of Camus who are interested in his political thought will wish to study the entirety of the volume *Actuelles: Ecrits politiques* in which "Neither Victims Nor Executioners" is included, along with several other essays from the 1946–48 period. In Camus's eyes, the end of World War II brought with it more problems than its conclusion had apparently solved. Most importantly, the realm of "abstraction" could no longer be limited to *one* specific plague against which people could struggle with some degree of common purpose. The post-war world, divided into ideological camps and seemingly on the brink of a nuclear holocaust, had outstripped the capacity of individuals to comprehend its complexities. The technological age that was about to begin was not congenial to Camus's Mediterranean philosophy, as we shall see in the next chapter. For the moment, it is necessary to see in the notion of "abstraction" not only a central (perhaps *the* central) issue in *The Plague,* but also a concept that will inform Camus's political thought continually—in fact, until the end of his life.

b. Paneloux's Sermons and the Problem of Religion

For those citizens of Oran who believed in a Christian God, the period of the plague was a particularly difficult ordeal. The atheist found in the epidemic the manifestation of some blind and malevolent force of nature that remained necessarily incomprehensible; the Christian, on the other hand, was tempted to see in its outbreak the clear sign of God's wrath. The "abstraction," in the mind of the believer, contained a message from on high that demanded his careful deciphering. The individual to whom the task of interpreting the divine signs fell was Paneloux, the intellectual and activist Jesuit priest.

In his first sermon (*Part Two, 95–102*), Paneloux evokes past historical occurrences of the disease, beginning with the plague visited upon Egypt by Jehovah that cleared the way for the Exodus of the Israelites under the leadership of Moses. Paneloux's point is that each time the plague returns, it is to humble nonbelievers and warn believers against the loosening of their faith. He begins his discourse with the portentous words: "Brethren, you are living in misfortune, brethren, you deserve your lot" (P 97). His purpose is to demonstrate that what seems incomprehensible to the human mind originates in the grand design of God. Furthermore, according to the priest, it is precisely *within* the destructiveness of the pestilence that the believing Christian can find "an exquisite ray of eternity" (P 101) that leads toward deliverance:

> this ray . . . manifests the will of God, which without fail transforms evil into good. Even today, through this progression of death, anguish, and lamentation, it guides us toward essential silence and toward the principle of all life. There, my brethren, is the immense consolation I wanted to bring you so that you might not only take away with you chastizing words, but also a message of conciliation (P Ibid.).

Readers of *The Myth of Sisyphus* will recognize here the logic of consolation that Camus had condemned in the Christian existentialists Chestov and Kierkegaard, the "metaphysical reversal" that transforms the fundamental absurdity of the human condition into a transcendentally grounded meaningfulness. At this early stage in the progression of the epidemic, Paneloux is able to appeal rather successfully to the conscience of his parishioners, and his sermon has a strong, bracing effect on the faith of his flock. When he delivers his second sermon, however (*Part Four,*

219–27), conditions have changed, and his further use of the same logic pushed to the extreme limit of its harshness falls largely on deaf ears. Between the time of the first sermon and the second, Paneloux, like all citizens of Oran, has lived surrounded by death; in particular, he has witnessed the agonizing death of Othon's young son. While standing at the child's bedside, he had to face the anger of Dr. Rieux, who had exclaimed, in an accusatory tone: "Now this child, at least, was innocent, you can't deny that!" (*P 216*). Paneloux's response—"But perhaps we must love what we cannot comprehend" (*P 217*)—provokes what is no doubt the most passionate outburst by Rieux in the novel: "No, my father . . . I have a different idea of love. And I will refuse to the death to love this creation in which children are tortured" (*P Ibid.*). In this instance, Rieux is uttering Camus's own personal opinion as a non-believing humanist, as the anti-existentialist theoretician of the absurd.

Paneloux shows courage in his second sermon in that he takes on directly the problem (or "scandal") of the death of innocent children and makes it his theme. It is as if he is speaking from the pulpit to Rieux, as if all his theological training and erudition are compressed into one argument in an implicit dialogue with his atheistic adversary. Once again, the logic is that of the "metaphysical reversal," but in this case the tone is more dramatic, more suffused with pathos. At the heart of his argument is an appeal to an all-or-nothing alternative: either one is a Christian or one is not; either one believes everything or nothing; if one's position vis-à-vis God is that of humility, such humility must be absolute; absolute faith and absolute humility presuppose that one accepts every manifestation of divine will, including the plague—otherwise one accepts nothing. Thus, in Paneloux's words (which are a very faithful echo of the Kierkegaardian "leap of faith"), as indirectly retranscribed by Rieux:

it was necessary to leap into the very heart of this inacceptable alternative that was offered us, precisely so that we might make our choice. The suffering of children was our bitter bread, but without this bread, our soul would perish of spiritual hunger (*P 224–25*).

Shortly after delivering his second sermon, Paneloux dies. He refuses all medical help and suffers in stoic silence. The man who has offered spiritual consolation to his parishioners does not accept the consolations of human science; his death is consequent, it follows the logic of his beliefs and actions. In the symmetrical juxtaposition of the two sermons at two radically different moments of the plague and in the confrontation between Rieux and Paneloux, Camus has granted a central position to religion in his novel. Although the author, like his narrator-protagonist, and in diametrical opposition to his foil Paneloux, refuses all forms of metaphysical consolation, he expresses clear admiration for a man who establishes his life on a strong moral foundation and who can live with the consequences of his choices. Like the classical playwright Corneille, who fills his tragedies with enemies who, in the end, can only have esteem for each other, Camus has created, in the Rieux-Paneloux dialogue, two antagonists who inescapably recognize each other's worth.

c. Tarrou and "The Hour of Friendship"

Toward the end of Part Four, at the very height of the novel's action, Camus inserts a scene between Dr. Rieux and Tarrou that constitutes both a crucial development on the multiple symbolic meanings of the plague and a welcome pause in the dramatic tension. Tarrou, Rieux and their associates have witnessed the suffering and death of innumerable individuals, and have reached the stage at which they are very nearly numb to the devastation of their environment. It is at this point that the two men enjoy what Tarrou calls an "hour of friendship"—an evening spent together away from the burdens of the day and their common service to the community (*P 244–55*).

Until this scene, Tarrou's past has been an enigma. The reader knows of him only through the shrewd and original observations of his diaries and through his faithful work in the Sanitary organization that he created. For the first time, as the novel reaches its crisis and dénouement, we hear Tarrou speak directly and unequivocally about his formative years. What he says is in the mode of a highly personal confession; yet what he reveals about himself has major implications for the overall meaning of *The Plague* as an aesthetic whole. We learn that Tarrou's father was a respected lawyer who, when he was not prosecuting criminals, enjoyed consulting railway timetables in his spare time. Significantly, he rarely traveled: what interested him were the multiple possible connections among places in the abstract, not the concrete experience of these places in their everyday reality. This fundamental trait of character—the love of abstraction—carried over into his professional life, as the young Tarrou was

110

to discover. One day, in an effort to impress his son and interest him in the future pursuit of law, the prosecutor invited him to the courtroom. There, in a dazzling display of legal logic and rhetorical brilliance, Tarrou's father successfully obtained the death penalty for a man whom Tarrou merely remembered in his physical insignificance, as a "sandy-haired owl" (P 248). Most impressive to the son was the father's use of the term "the accused" to designate the man he was condemning to death; by using this expression, the prosecutor effectively eliminated the individuality and humanity of the man on trial.

For Tarrou, the remembrance of this one childhood scene was to remain at the center of his later political and social consciousness. In essence, all of his adult life was to be a revolt against his father's arrogant use of abstraction; and this abstraction derived from the latter's sure knowledge of his own innocence, in contradistinction to the clear guilt of "the accused." What Tarrou learned from his day in court is that no one human can presume to be innocent, that no person can arrogate the power to condemn another to die on the basis of a supposed ethical superiority. From this initial discovery, Tarrou concludes, first: "none of us could make the slightest gesture in this world without the risk of causing death" (P 250–51). Second, expressed in metaphorical terms, this meant that none of us could pretend to be healthy in a moral sense: we were all, in Tarrou's language, *des pestiférés*—carriers of the plague.

Unlike the majority of the inhabitants of Oran, for whom the plague represented an unjust intrusion from some mysterious "outside" or "beyond," a calamitous descent of evil into a luminous world, Tarrou knew, before ever reaching Oran, that all of us carry the plague within us, as a fundamental constitutive part of our being. Hence his only apparently paradoxical assertion: "What is natural is the microbe. All the rest—health, integrity, purity, if you will—is the effect of the will, of a will that must never cease to be active" (*P 251*). Tarrou's metaphorical use of the word "plague" to signify the evil within each of us, our subservience to the seductions of "abstraction" in its various guises (including that abstraction in reasoning that justifies the death penalty), adds a level of connotative potential to the allegory of the novel. To reduce *The Plague* to a mere literary transposition of World War II is to overlook the pertinence of Tarrou's reflections: indeed, if the plague that descends on Oran "is" the War, it is only too easy to reduce the entirety of Camus's fiction to a simple mechanical allegory of Good (Rieux, Tarrou, the Sanitary team as Resistance fighters) versus Evil (the epidemic as objective correlative of Hitler's holocaust). But if we take Tarrou's observations seriously, we discover a more sobering message: namely, that the inherent tendency toward evil that exists in each human being must be countered daily by an act of the will. Innocence being impossible and, in the strictest sense, irretrievable, the attempt to live morally (i.e., our effort *not* to carry the plague) becomes a properly Sisyphian task. Camus has progressed a great distance from the Romantic pathos of *The Stranger,* in which Meursault could proclaim his essential innocence until the moment of his "unjustified" execution. In *The Plague,* although Tarrou has killed no Arab on a beach, he knows that his every

112

action contains the potential for death. The world of *The Stranger* was that of an individual pursuing his existence in a solitary daydream state; the world of *The Plague* is that of a community in which each individual must adopt an active wakefulness so as not to lapse into the tempting habits of the prosecutor standing in judgment over his neighbor.

At the end of the scene, to seal their friendship, Rieux and Tarrou take a nocturnal swim in the ocean. In this one exceptional moment of respite, human solidarity becomes a reality. The silent communication that acts as a bond between the two men also serves as a poetic counterbalance to the stark philosophy Tarrou had expounded earlier in the chapter: by merely being together *as* friends enveloped in the natural force of the tides, Rieux and Tarrou incorporate the promise of deliverance from the abstractions of the plague. As they swim together, side by side in the same rhythm, their conjugated movements illustrate the possibility of overcoming the "permanent exile" (*P 252*) to which Tarrou said he had condemned himself. This promise or possibility emerges in the only lyrical moment of the novel, and that moment is short-lived. Yet its very fragility haunts the remainder of Rieux's chronicle and stands as a reminder of the hope that never quite disappears from a city permeated with death.

d. Narration: The Art of Bearing Witness

From a technical standpoint, the most unusual feature of *The Plague* is its masking, until the final chapter of Part Five, of the narrator's identity. It is only in the concluding pages of the novel that Dr. Rieux steps forward to assume responsibility for the account we have just read and to justify his procedure. On the simplest level, the choice of Rieux as narrator is logical in that he is in a position, as medical doctor, to observe the ravages of the plague first-hand. Further, as a member of the Sanitary brigades organized by Tarrou, he is able to describe his fellow-citizens from close range. And finally, in his struggle with separation and exile (his wife, being away from Oran in a clinic, can offer him no support, and he is deprived of news on her condition), he shares the suffering of those whom he helps on a daily basis. Rieux explains (*P 302–03*) that he has tried to be as objective as possible: he has attempted not to "mix in a direct way his own personal impressions with the thousand voices of those afflicted with the plague." Thus, his method of narration can most properly be described as a *témoignage,* or bearing witness. In *The Plague,* we are far removed from the personal tone of *The Stranger* or from the confessional hyperbole of *The Fall.* To bear witness is to efface oneself in order to better express the physical and spiritual state of an entire community. And in so doing, in Rieux's own words, "he wished to be reunited with his fellow-citizens in the only certainties they had in common, which are love, suffering, and exile." Paradoxically, therefore, it is through a sober, neutral style that does not call attention to itself that Rieux is best able to reach the emotional depths within which the people of Oran were forced to descend during the period of the plague.

At the moment of deliverance from the epidemic, which Rieux describes in terms that must have brought to mind the Liberation of Paris to many Frenchmen in 1947, the desire for personal happiness reasserts itself powerfully, as couples and families are united once again. In evoking one last time the essential differences between the sacrifice of self that characterized the era of the plague and the yearning for pleasure that had been dormant but always present in all individuals, the narrator opposes the crucial terms *exil* (exile) and *patrie* (homeland). With forced imprisonment or exile now a thing of the past, the citizens of Oran begin to think of their *patrie,* which can be found "beyond the walls of this suffocated city. It [*la patrie*] was in these sweet-smelling thickets on the hillsides, in the ocean, the free land and the weight of love" (*P 299*). This opposition—between exile and a certain homeland or "kingdom"—will inform the last series of short stories written by Camus in 1957. In *The Plague,* the novelist chose to depict a situation in which the promise of a return to one's personal homeland is kept in near-constant abeyance by the stifling omnipresence of an epidemic signifying the absolute of human evil. Through Dr. Rieux's narrative conscientiousness, through his refusal to do more than bear witness, we as readers can never succumb to the premature hope of an escape from exile. Yet in his later works —in the essays and fictions of the 1950s—Camus returns to the problem of the relative place (or value) of his two oppositional terms, in an attempt to justify philosophically and ground ethically the urge for a homeland that inhabits us all, and that disappears only briefly, when we fall prey to the catastrophes of our own making. At the very end of his narrative commentary, Dr. Rieux suggests that although Tarrou's refusal of all consolations, his willingness to live in a world completely devoid of hope, could be considered admirable, nevertheless for the majority of people such an attitude is impossible. In Rieux's consciousness there is room not only for the events of the present in their current horror, but also for a world of sea and sky that can never be erased as long as human beings have the courage to refuse the enslavement brought on by the plagues of which they are, unfortunately, the carriers.

CHAPTER FIVE

L'Homme révolté (*The Rebel*) and *La Chute* (*The Fall*)

I. *The Rebel*

Published in October 1951, *The Rebel* is not only Camus's longest work, but perhaps his most ambitious as well. The earliest notes for *The Rebel* are from the year 1942, and since that time Camus had returned to the elaboration of his treatise on a regular basis, changing its thematic emphases and progressively expanding its scope. Just as *The Myth of Sisyphus* provided the philosophical underpinnings for the Cycle of the Absurd, in the same way *The Rebel* was to ground and justify the central notion of *révolte* as elaborated in the novel *The Plague* and the play *Les Justes*. Although it is not absolutely necessary to have read *The Rebel* before undertaking an analysis of *The Plague,* nevertheless several of the major themes developed in the philosophical essay in a conceptual way mirror the central issues of the novel that had been published four years before. In an important sense, what Dr. Rieux does in *The Plague* constitutes an enactment of the ideas on which *The Rebel* is founded.

As we shall see in more detail later in this chapter, *The Rebel* was controversial from the start. Its general theses as well as a number of its particular observations offended devout Christians, doctrinaire Marxists, surrealists, and existentialists. What Camus proposed in his treatise was a highly personal view of the place and essential role of human beings in the world—a view that did not accommodate the religious, aesthetic and ideological systems that were vying for dominance among European intellectuals. As we read *The Rebel,* we must keep in mind that the historical context and political landscape in which it was composed differ markedly from ours today. In the late forties and early fifties, Europe continued to suffer from what one might call the "after-shock" of World War II. National economies were being rebuilt slowly and painfully; governments, laws, and constitutions were put to the test; artists began to re-examine their function within an increasingly mechanized and technological world. In this transitional phase, it was tempting for intellectuals to turn toward a system of thought for solutions to the manifold problems of the day. Thus, the existentialist Jean-Paul Sartre and his coterie of admirers moved increasingly toward a rigid form of Marxism and interpreted the particular political events of the period through its political/economical grid. The originality of *The Rebel* lies in its refusal to join any camp, in its dogged undermining of the arrogant will to power on which so many political systems are built, whether knowingly or unconsciously. In short, Camus recognizes within politics (and within religion and certain forms of aesthetic conceptions as well) a desire to win back for humankind a state of happiness or innocence that had been lost through the violence of historical evolution, but he also finds, in the movement from political theorizing to concrete social action, a constant perversion of ideals, such that the initial aspirations on which the political system is founded disappear under the accumulated weight of betrayals, rivalries, deception, and the diverse abuses of power.

Like *The Myth of Sisyphus, The Rebel* poses problems to readers uninitiated in philosophy and in the history of European ideas. Although Camus is always clear in his method of presenting and developing the central concepts of his own essay, he presupposes that we know something about the Age of Enlightenment, the development of German Idealism, the writings of Marx and Lenin, and the general outline of Christian theology. If this should not be the case, some sections of *The Rebel* may seem obscure because they allude to ideas or to historical facts that Camus considers to be common currency in the European context, but that may have less immediate resonance for the nonspecialist contemporary American reader. With this state of affairs in mind, I shall divide my commentary of *The Rebel* into two parts. In the first of these, I shall trace the order of Camus's argument through its various stages, emphasizing thematic continuities that link the sections and that guarantee the ultimate unity of the treatise. My purpose here is not to provide an exhaustive analysis of a complex and detailed text, but rather to trace a broad outline of the essay's development that the reader can use as a preliminary guide for his own further investigations. In the second part, I shall examine briefly and selectively some key interpretive issues that arise from the controversial and somewhat idiosyncratic conclusion of the essay, and that continue to play a pivotal role in the evolution of Camus's thought after *The Rebel*.

1. Structure and General Content

In this portion of my commentary, I shall follow the progression of the essay step by step, making use of Camus's own section-headings.

a. Introduction (15–24)

Camus begins his treatise by observing that the world in which we live today is characterized by "logical crime" (*HR 15*), that is, a form of violence that one human being visits upon another in the name of some ideological principle. Gone are the days in which tyrannical rulers burned down villages and offered up human sacrifices to the multitudes in barbarous triumphant games; contemporary society would recoil from such spectacles, but seems to require a more convoluted form of crime, which Camus describes in striking paradoxical terms:

> concentration camps under the banner of freedom, massacres justified by the love of mankind or the taste for the superhuman, are disabling to human judgment. When crime adorns itself with the spoils of innocence, by a curious reversal that is characteristic of our time, it is up to innocence to justify itself. The ambitious project of this essay is to accept and to examine this strange challenge (*HR 16*).

According to Camus, the appalling phenomenon of the twentieth-century concentration camp deserves scrutiny not merely because of the suffering and deaths it produced, but also (perhaps especially) because it seems to have derived logically from a specific political ideology. Because Hitler and his minions had espoused a vaguely Nietzschean ideal of the supremacy of a Master Race, because the achievement of racial "purity" was predicated on the elimination of "impure elements," it became possible for the theoreticians of Nazism to manipulate the minds of their followers to such an extent that the latter could justify the death camps as a necessary "cleansing" step toward a final utopian goal rather than see the camps for what they were: namely, a monument to man's descent into bestiality and amorality. This kind of grotesque reasoning is what Camus calls the logic of "curious reversals" that characterizes our modernity. As he surveys the contemporary political horizon, Camus notes that all the major ideologies lay claim to the ideals of freedom and justice, but that in too many cases the concrete political practice of governments consists not only of depriving individuals of their rights, but also of imprisoning and killing those members of society who dissent and deviate from established norms.

In the most general terms, the purpose of Camus's essay will be to determine "whether innocence, when translated into action, cannot avoid killing" (*Ibid.*). In other words, is it inevitable that even those political systems based upon the highest ethical principles are doomed to degenerate, via the conflicts and compromises of the historical process, into a monstrous parody of their original theoretical formulation? This is the major question posed by *The Rebel,* and Camus's response occupies the entirety of the treatise.

121

In the last three pages of the Introduction, Camus alludes to the method he had adopted for *The Myth of Sisyphus,* which he compares explicitly to the stance of "methodical doubt" (*HR 23*) as practiced by the classical French philosopher René Descartes in his influential *Meditations.* Camus asserts that the feeling of the absurd that inhabits the modern individual, like methodical doubt, leaves each of us facing a blank slate, or *tabula rasa.* To live within the absurd is to face an apparent impasse. At the same time, however, the cry of protest issued against the absurdity of human existence, this impassioned utterance of human *révolte,* is itself not subject to doubt. Thus at the very beginning of his essay, Camus establishes a strong link between his two philosophical works. *The Rebel* will not be an overcoming or overturning of *The Myth of Sisyphus,* but rather a continuation of its essential preoccupations. The point of departure remains the recognition of absurdity, but now Camus wishes to examine "the first and the only evidence that is given to me within the experience of the absurd, [which] is *la révolte* (revolt, rebellion)" (*Ibid.*). Following is Camus's concise and suggestive definition of revolt—its distinguishing traits and its central importance in the struggle for freedom and coherence:

Revolt is born in the spectacle of unreason [*déraison*], in the presence of an unjust and incomprehensible condition. But its blind aspiration lays claim to order in the midst of chaos and to unity at the very heart of that which flees and disappears (*Ibid.*).

In the succeeding chapters of his book, Camus will analyze the phenomenon of revolt in its various historical guises and will seek to demonstrate not only its resilient reappearances throughout modern European history, but also the ways in which the aspiration to unity that inhabits *l'homme révolté* (the rebel, the human being in revolt) has given way to possessive dominance, the arbitrary exercise of power, and totalitarian ambition.

b. *L'homme révolté* (The Rebel) (27–38)

At the beginning of the second section of the essay, Camus reminds us that the word "revolt," in its Latin etymological sense, means a "turning around." The slave who revolts against his master is a person who refuses to take a further step under the whip, and who turns around in a movement of defiance and self-affirmation. In so doing, however, the slave become rebel does not act in his own name, but on behalf of a good (*un bien*) or a value (*une valeur*) that surpasses his limited individual fate and that binds him to the human community at large (*HR 30*). (It is worth noting in this context that just as *The Plague* differs from *The Stranger* in its emphasis on the community rather than the individual, in the same way *The Rebel* extends the analyses of *The Myth of Sisyphus* into a prolonged reflection on the place of the human being within political and social units.) Camus affirms that the value in the name of which the rebel acts *pre-exists* his every action. This means that the movement of revolt is not arbitrary or morally experimental; it is not the mere overturning of one system by another, but the ethically grounded enactment of a claim to human dignity. As such, revolt in its Camusian definition implies the existence of a *human nature:*

it is crucial to note that this value that pre-exists all action contradicts those purely historically determined philosophies according to which value is conquered (if it can be conquered at all) at the conclusion of action. The analysis of revolt leads at least to the suspicion that there is a human nature, as the Greeks conceived of it, contrary to the postulates of contemporary thought. Why rebel if there is nothing of inherent value and permanence worth preserving? (*Ibid.*).

Here, in a nutshell, Camus foreshadows much of his argument in the lengthier sections that follow. The allusion to "historically determined philosophies" is a thinly veiled reference to twentieth-century Marxism and its reliance on the Hegelian system, which, according to Camus, glorified history at the expense of moral values. The essayist's assertion that there is a human nature "contrary to the postulates of contemporary thought" is most likely directed against Sartrian existentialism, according to which existence precedes essence (that is, all general and abstract notions such as "human nature" are viewed as non-determinative of the human being's concrete existential situation in Sartre's philosophical system). Thus, although the issues with which Camus is dealing at the beginning of *The Rebel* might seem purely and objectively philosophical to the modern American reader, they were polemically charged at the time of the text's publication. Adherents of Marxism and existentialism did not have to wait for the broadside attacks of the essay's later chapters to understand that Camus had no sympathy for their theories.

In the final pages of the second section, Camus distances himself from religious thought ("Man in revolt is a man situated before or after the sacred who lays claim to a human order where all answers are human, that is, reasonably formulated"—*HR 36*) and establishes the central importance of *limits* for his conception of revolt. Indeed, since an individual rebels not in his own name but for the sake of humankind, since his actions lead toward a strengthening of solidarity within the community, these actions must respect "that limit where human beings, in joining together, begin to be" (*HR 37*). As we shall see in the conclusion of the essay, Camus will equate the notion of *limite* with classical Greek philosophy and with the Greek sense of human nature. Revolt, therefore, is a turning around, a refusal to proceed in the path of slavery, an affirmation of human freedom that transcends the individual without glorifying his supremacy or superiority over the fellow-humans for whom he struggles. In moving from the level of the absurd to that of revolt, "the evil that tormented solitary man becomes a collective *plague* [*peste collective*]" (*HR 38*). When Camus concludes, in Cartesian terms, "Je me révolte, donc nous sommes" ["I rebel, therefore we are"] (*Ibid.*), he is expressing the essential message of *The Rebel* in a concentrated formula while describing the actions of Dr. Rieux and his "sanitary formations" in *The Plague:* in both cases, the evil of the world is symbolized as an epidemic against which only collective intervention, only the collaboration of people bound together in a common cause, can lift the human condition above suffering and violence, and beyond the cyclical alternations of mastery and servitude.

c. *La révolte métaphysique* (Metaphysical Revolt) (57–135)

In the first sentence of the third section, Camus writes: "Metaphysical revolt is the movement by which a man rises up against his condition and all of creation. It is metaphysical because it calls into question the ends of man and of creation" (*HR 57*). Whereas the slave protests his treatment within the conditions allotted him by his master, the human individual who rebels "metaphysically" protests against his condition *as* human being. In the lengthy argument that constitutes the third section of the essay, Camus traces schematic portraits of people and personages (legendary, fictional, and real) who are famous for their exemplary acts of rebellion. He begins with accounts from Greek mythology and from the Bible, then discusses such disparate figures as the Marquis de Sade, the "Dandies" of the nineteenth century, Dostoevsky's character Ivan Karamazov, Friedrich Nietzsche (the link of his philosophy to revolt as well as the distortions of his ideas by the Nazis), the rebel poets Lautréamont and Rimbaud, and the surrealists (their love poetry and their questionable aesthetic theories). According to Camus's interpretation, the thread that links this gallery of rebellious actors and attitudes is woven in violence and the pursuit of power. From the first recorded instance of rebellion in the Bible—Cain's rage against God's preference of Abel, an anger that resulted in murder—through the numbing enumeration of cruelty and torture contained in Sade's fictions, to the grotesque realization of Nietzschean "super-humanity" in the Nazi concentration camps, the revolt of the individual against his limited condition (in Camus's terms, against the absurdity of existence) has led, all too often, to the abyss of inhumanity and crime.

In each case Camus examines, he finds the expression of the same bitter irony: the movement of revolt, which contains within itself the potential for a strengthening of human solidarity, seems to reverse itself, to turn into its opposite. Thus, in the instance of the Marquis de Sade, whose entire literary work centers on the liberation of desire from all constraints, the exasperated attempts to achieve absolute revolt yield a world of masters and slaves, produce an unending series of stifling rooms, chateaux and fortresses. Because, in Camus's words, Sadian revolt has forgotten "the truth of its origins," its consequences become "a closed totality, universal crime, the aristocracy of cynicism and the will to apocalypse" (*HR 69*). Camus sees a direct link between the outrageous imaginings of Sade and the reality of twentieth-century history: it is as if the most unbelievable fiction had become reality in our time of police states and prison camps. In the end, the more humankind loses all belief in God (in a divinity that encompasses and justifies the state of the world), the more it tends to make of its environment a vast fortress, the more its political and social structures imitate the confinement of a prison.

At the conclusion of the third section, Camus makes explicit the three-stage process by which revolt degenerates into crime:

1. In the beginning, the rebel sees that he is inferior, finds that he is in a position of servitude.
2. Wishing to liberate himself from tyranny, he "turns around" and revolts.

3. Having revolted, he *forgets* the origins of his revolt (the pursuit of equality and dignity) and, "according to the law of a spiritual imperialism, now he marches toward dominion over the world through infinitely repeated murder" (*HR 135*).

As the third section draws to a close, Camus leaves us with the open question: is it possible to conceive of revolt in a form that does not follow this seemingly inevitable pattern of betrayal and destruction? In other words, can we imagine a revolt that remembers and is faithful to its origins?

d. *La révolte historique* (Historical Revolt) (139–314)

In the fourth and longest section of his treatise, Camus examines the application and realization of political theories within the concrete world of historical fact. He begins his analysis with an overview of the French Revolution, proceeds to a schematic interpretation of certain aspects of Hegel's philosophy, then selectively discusses examples of what he calls "individual terrorism" (from Russian history before 1917) and "State terrorism" (essentially Marxism in its post-1917 manifestations). This part of *The Rebel* was the most controversial at the moment of its publication because of its direct attack on Marxist-Leninist doctrine, which had gained in prestige among leftist French intellectuals during and immediately after World War II. At the same time, Camus opened himself to the criticism of academic specialists in the fields of philosophy and history by his perhaps excessively schematic presentation of complex philosophical and historical issues. Although it was not the essayist's purpose to provide a definitive interpretation of the French Revolution in thirty pages or a "new" account of Hegel in the same short space, his detractors capitalized on the rapidity of his argument in their condemnation of his general thesis.

At the beginning of the section, Camus makes an important distinction—between the notions of revolt and revolution. In a sense, the entirety of "Historical Revolt" is devoted to an examination of the degeneration of revolt into revolution—the way in which the originary movement of "turning around," in becoming politicized, loses its meaning. In Camus's precise formulation:

> The movement of revolt, from the beginning, reaches an impasse. It is only an incoherent act of witnessing. Revolution, on the other hand, begins with an idea. Precisely, revolution is the insertion of the idea into historical experience, whereas revolt is only the movement that leads from individual experience to the idea (*HR 140*).

It would be difficult to overestimate the value of this initial distinction for the totality of *The Rebel*. What Camus calls "the insertion of the idea into historical experience" defines not only the ideological debates of the French Revolution, but also Lenin's use of Marxist tenets to influence the outcome of his country's class struggle, and Mao's use of self-quotation (via the dissemination of the "Little Red Book") to drive the Chinese Cultural Revolution of the sixties and seventies. The ultimate purpose of all modern revolutions, according to Camus, is to "fashion the world in a theoretical framework" (*Ibid.*). Of major concern to the essayist is that this fashioning, this bending of concrete reality to fit a preordained scheme, has as its essential consequence the enslavement of the individual. In our modern age of radical scepticism, in which Nietzsche's provocative formula "God is dead" takes on a profound, quasi-literal resonance, Camus asserts that political theories, especially those that proclaim the inevitable liberation of the individual at the end of an historical process, have replaced God, and have reduced each human to a state of abject worshipful passivity in the face of an abstract, ill-defined fate.

What Camus criticizes, both in the philosophical works of the German Idealist G.W.F. Hegel and in the application, by Karl Marx, of Hegelian concepts to economic and political reality, is the "divinization" of history: that is, all human actions receive their legitimation *ex post facto,* once historical evolution has reached its culmination—in "Absolute Knowledge" (Hegel) or the perfected, achieved Communist State (Marx). Camus does not question the intellectual rigor of the Hegelian and Marxian systems, nor does he condemn out of hand their idealizing and utopian dimensions, but he finds in them the origins of modern-day totalitarian and terrorist States. The reason the works of Hegel and Marx produced the monstrosities of our current political regimes can be found in the permanent shelving or deferring of human values—a logical outcome of the belief in the finality of revealed historical truth:

> Cynicism, the divinization of history and of the material realm, individual terror and the crimes of the State, these inordinate consequences will spring up,

armed to the teeth, from an equivocal conception of the world that entrusts to history alone the task of producing values and the truth. If nothing can be conceived of clearly before the final illumination of the truth at the end of time, all action is arbitrary, and force alone will reign (*HR 189*).

The final pages of the section (on "State Terrorism" and "Rational Terror") contain not only Camus's harshest critique of Marxism and of Christian theology, but also a brief exposition of the personal views he will develop at the conclusion of the essay. In his contrasting of the ancient Greek notion of cyclical Becoming to the Marxist conception of historical evolution, and in his juxtaposition of the Christian and Marxist ideals of mastery over nature to the Greek precept of obedience to natural laws, Camus makes clear where his own preference lies, and he foreshadows the importance of the classical sense of Measure (of harmony between man and his surroundings) that he draws from *Nuptials* for elaboration at the close of *The Rebel*. In the final pages of "Historical Revolt" Camus reminds us that the rebel seeks unity: that is, his act of rebellion is a search for coherence in a world whose appearance is disorderly, chaotic. What the rebel does not seek, however, is totality. It is the arrogance of the modern individual that has propelled him, in his desire for total mastery over his political and natural environment, toward the enslavement of prison camps and the violence of ideologically driven warfare (*HR 300–301*). One senses, as the section draws to a close, that Camus's own projected vision of life within the modern world will be more modest.

e. *Révolte et Art* (Rebellion and Art) (317–345)

As I pointed out in Chapter One of this study, although Camus (unlike Sartre) cannot be considered a theoretician of literature, his views on artistic creation are clear, cogent, and coherent. In general terms, one can say that Camus avoided the extremes of excessive formalism on the one hand and of didacticism on the other: his own writing was based neither on the ideal of art for art's sake, nor on the subservience of form to message, but rather on a careful balancing of ethical or philosophical content with structural and stylistic constraints. Art relates to the world (it is not sufficient unto itself or self-referential), it points to the reality in which we live, to a specifically human universe, but it does so precisely *by* and *in* the creation of a style. At the beginning of the fifth section of his essay, Camus writes:

> Art also is this movement that exalts and negates at the same time ... Creation simultaneously postulates unity and refuses the world. But it refuses the world because of what the world lacks yet, on occasion, is. Revolt allows itself to be observed here, outside of history, in its pure state, in its primitive complication. Thus art should give us a final perspective on the content of revolt (*HR 317*).

For Camus, therefore, art is not confined to the giving and receiving of aesthetic pleasure, but is itself an exemplary form of *révolte*. In a direct prefiguration of his Nobel Prize *Conférence* pronounced in Uppsala in 1957, Camus states here that art must both seek unity (through the rigor of style) and "refuse" the world. This refusal should not be confused with a hiding or an avoidance, however. In a later passage, the essayist asserts that "art contests reality but does not shrink from it" (*HR 323*). Most crucially, art can lead us to the very origins of revolt insofar as it "attempts to lend form to a value that flees in perpetual becoming, but that the artist intuits and attempts to wrest from history" (*Ibid.*).

In the sub-sections "The Novel and Revolt," "Revolt and Style," and "Creation and Revolution," Camus makes increasingly explicit the link between artistic creation and human values. Once again, he emphasizes the existence of a human nature that transcends mere historical process, and he sees in authentic art a privileged means to the assuaging of "the hunger for freedom and dignity that resides in the heart of everyone" (*HR 345*). In positing an intimate connection between revolt and art, in granting to the creative act the power of negating but also of transforming the world and of contributing to the liberation of humankind, Camus shows himself to be a humanist in the classical sense of the term—a thinker who refuses to deny the centrality and essential worth of the individual, despite the ever-expanding claims made on that individual by competing ideological systems.

f. *La pensée de midi* (Mediterranean Thought) (349–382)

In the final section of his essay, Camus provides both a recapitulation of his major themes and a provocative solution to the problem of revolt expressed in the form of a myth. He begins by reminding us that his own notion of *révolte* is incompatible with the perpetual alternations of mastery and slavery that have characterized modern political systems despite the lofty claims of freedom and justice made by these systems. He states that the human being in revolt, the rebel (*l'homme révolté*), is not passively subservient to the force of historical change, but has the same relation to history as does the artist to the reality he seeks to depict (*HR 361*). Thus Camus implies that the human being of the twentieth century, far from being merely a component of "the masses" or "the people," is capable of transforming and ameliorating his world.

Central to Camus's argument as he reaches the height of his peroration are the key notions of measure and limits, which had been mentioned previously in passing but without ample development. As he had done in the last chapter of *The Myth of Sisyphus,* when he had found in the legends of ancient Greece an exemplary fable to illustrate his philosophical position, similarly in *The Rebel* he has recourse to early Greek literature for his final demonstration of the values inherent in his conception of revolt. Camus recalls that the pre-Socratic philosopher Heraclitus, famous for his reflections on temporal flux or becoming (*le devenir*), nevertheless set clear bounds for the apparently perpetual flow of time: he symbolized these bounds or limits by the figure of Nemesis, goddess of measure, fatal enemy of all immoderate or excessive human actions (*HR 369–370*). As he reaches the conclusion of his treatise, Camus equates the wisdom of measure (*mesure*) with ancient Greek thought and opposes it to the folly of excess and inordinate action (*démesure*), which he links to the modern German philosophical tradition. Further, he establishes a poetic analogy between "Germanic dreams" and midnight, whereas he finds in the moderate conceptions of Greece the expression of what he calls *la pensée solaire*—solar thought, thought illuminated by reason *(HR 372- 373)*. As we read the final paragraphs of *The Rebel,* we discover the degree to which his mature philosophical essay remains faithful to the exalted prose poetry of *Nuptials*. In both works, Camus asserts the primacy of Mediterranean culture—a culture that originates in ancient Greece, but that extends to those modern-day European, middle-Eastern, and North African countries that lie on the rim of Western civilization's "Middle Sea."

Camus's dramatic opposition of North to South, of "the Germanic" to "the Greek," of "midnight" to "noonday illumination" is, of course, questionable in its extreme apodictic formulation. Camus holds Europe (northern Europe) responsible for the ills of the twentieth century, and calls for a return to Mediterranean thought as a means to recovering the authentic sense of values that resides in his own notion of revolt. In so doing, however, the essayist sounds, for a brief moment, culturally chauvinistic, ethnocentric in a distinctly unenlightened way:

> There is, certainly, within the Russian people an exemplary sense of sacrifice that should inspire Europe, and in America a necessary constructive power. But the youth of the world is still to be found around the same shores. Thrown into an ignoble Europe where, deprived of beauty and of friendship, the proudest of races is dying, we Mediterraneans continue to live in the same light. At the heart of the European night, solar thought [*la pensée solaire*] . . . waits for its new dawn *(HR 375)*.

In this passage and in a number of the political essays Camus was composing during the same period, one senses the frustration of a writer who wished to hark back to an earlier time, but who was intuitively aware of major geopolitical changes that had been brought about by World War II. The two powers Camus mentions in passing—Russia and America (i.e., the Soviet Union and the United States)—had entered into a Cold War and were dominating the political landscape. Neither northern Europe nor the countries of the Mediterranean basin could lay claim to a central position in the historical evolution of the 1950s. One senses, therefore, that Camus's appeal to cultural unity and centrality was not so much an objectively formulated statement of a personal philosophical conviction as a passionate defensive or rear-guard action against the displacement of culture from its Greek sources toward the unimaginable, exotic shores of "America" and "Russia." In the world of the 1980s and 1990s, the new shores of the Pacific basin add to the decentralization of cultural hegemony. From our modern-day perspective, the very appeal to *one* origin of philosophy and enlightenment appears suspect, given the cultural relativism that defines our age of planetary technology.

2. Interpretive Issues

The purpose of the preceding paragraph was not to invalidate the entirety of Camus's philosophical enterprise in *The Rebel,* but rather to indicate that its conclusion contains perhaps more nostalgia for a world irrevocably lost than it holds promise for any future

solution to the evils that continue to afflict human beings in the late twentieth century. What Camus writes
in all the pages that lead up to his evocation of a Mediterranean unity, however, is not only intellectually
provocative and rigorous in its mode of presentation,
but also prophetic and uncannily relevant to the geo-
politics of the late 1980s.

At the time of its publication, as I have indicated in
passing, *The Rebel* drew protests and expressions of
outrage from the adherents of various systematic
modes of thought or belief—from Marxists, existentialists, surrealists, and Christians. This was inevitable,
since the polemical thrust of the essay was directed
against systems as such—against the abuses that arise
when an individual's aspirations to unity and coherence become subsumed within an all-powerful ideological edifice. Camus's definition of revolt, with its
emphasis on measure and moderation, with its recognition of the limits that must be respected so that my
act of rebellion does not interfere with or negate the
rebellion of another human—this definition that met
with the strongest possible resistance in 1951 has become implicit in many of the most far-reaching political reforms of the 1980s. The transformation of the
relations between management and trade unions in
several countries—from that of confrontation (management as "master" versus the union as "slave") to
cooperation (collaboration between the two groups in
both production and allocation of salary and bene-
fits)—depends on passing beyond the alternation of repression and revolution and on achieving the balance
between one person's rights and another's responsibili-

ties. Similarly, Mikhail Gorbachev's notions of *glasnost* (openness) and *perestroika* (restructuring) are challenging to the Soviet system insofar as they assert the existence of individual human values and the constructiveness of dialogue in the face of bureaucratic inertia and ideological monologue. The bankruptcy of Marxist-inspired Communism in Poland and East Germany and its redefinition in Hungary derive from the failure of "permanent revolution" to be more than the enslavement of the many by the privileged card-carrying few of the Party. Camus's clear distinction between revolt and revolution foreshadows the transformations that have swept not only Eastern Europe, but China as well. Camus recognized that to live in today's world requires an attitude or stance of *révolte,* that without adopting this stance we risk succumbing to passivity and accepting injustice; on the other hand, the extension of revolt into revolution brings on the hardening of bureaucratic structures and the beginning of the end of freedom.

Despite its faults—its bulkiness, its rapid and sometimes excessively assured arguments—*The Rebel* stands at the center not only of Camus's post-War literary production, but also of European thought. In 1951, when intellectuals looked to dogmas and fixed ideologies for the solutions to the contadictions of the world, *The Rebel* seemed irrelevant and out of place. After the publication of Aleksandr Solzhenitsyn's *The Gulag Archipelago* in the late 60s and early 70s, and after the "Prague Spring" of 1968, Camus's essay could be reread as a predictive statement of the excesses of imperial design and of the crimes against humanity born of a regime's arrogance in its disrespect for the individual. With *The Rebel,* Camus had accomplished the opposite of what he had achieved with *The Plague:* he had written an unpopular book, a volume completely out-of-season that would be vindicated only after his death. In the claustrophobic intellectual world of Paris, Camus would pay the price for his dismantling of the fashionable received opinions of the day.

II. *The Fall*

In late 1951 and during the early months of 1952, *The Rebel* was a much-discussed topic in French literary and philosophical circles. After the success of *The Plague,* Camus was ill-prepared for the incomprehending and occasionally violent reactions his treatise caused. On the one hand, he had trouble understanding why representatives of the conservative press admired his new work (especially since it contained much explicit criticism of Christian dogma), and on the other hand, he could not fathom the virulence with which the existentialists attacked his ideas. For some time, careful readers of Camus had known that his central preoccupations most often did not converge with those of Sartre or the existentialist camp, but the non-specialized reading public continued to speak of Camus and Sartre in the same breath, as twin representatives of a new literary order in France. The publication of *The Rebel* proved to be a convenient pretext for Sartre to consummate a clean break with Camus, and this break made the headlines even in the least intellectually inclined of Parisian newspapers.

In the May 1952 issue of *Les Temps Modernes,* the left-wing political and philosophical review published under Sartre's directorship, appeared an intelligent but abrasive and negative assessment of *The Rebel* written by a certain Francis Jeanson, a disciple of Sartre and author in his own right of rigorous academic books on modern philosophical thought. Jeanson took Camus to task for the vagueness of his ideological persuasions, for his superficial treatment of German Idealism and Marxism, and for his appeal to a Mediterranean *mesure*. The review, although excessively harsh in certain passages, was nevertheless well-written, and we know that it hurt Camus. The controversy continued and took on greater proportions when, in the August 1952 issue of *Les Temps Modernes,* appeared not only Camus's detailed response to Jeanson, but also a response to Camus's response written by Jean-Paul Sartre (who correctly recognized in the criticized essayist's rejoinders to Jeanson barbs directed against his own philosophical positions).

From our present-day, conveniently retrospective vantage point, it is easy to say that the break between Camus and Sartre (which lasted until Camus's death in January 1960) was inevitable. Ever since the end of World War II, the political persuasions of the two men had become increasingly divergent, and the works they produced in the literary arena could no longer be subsumed within some imagined common denominator. It seems equally clear, however, that the abruptness of the break came as a very unpleasant surprise to Camus and affected him deeply. He felt himself (rightly, in fact) to be ostracized and marginalized in certain circles of Parisian literary society. He became depressed, and between 1952 and 1956 only short political and journalistic essays appeared in his name. The

debate with Sartre and the Sartrians had not only isolated him, but had caused him to question the validity
of his own writing and especially of his literary work.

The publication in 1956 of *The Fall* dispelled any
premature notions concerning the demise of Camus's
literary talent. In a tightly structured imaginative fable centered in an examination of human duplicity remarkable for its mixture of lucidity and ferocious wit,
Camus made his return to center stage both assertive
and enigmatic. Of all Camus's texts, *The Fall* is the
most resistant to our understanding as readers, for two
essential reasons: (1) it is highly personal; its rhetorical mode is that of a monological confession; and (2) it
eludes our grasp by alluding to numerous other works
of literature in the Western tradition, from the Bible
through Dante to Dostoevsky, to such a degree that
we have difficulty separating levels of meaning in an
effort to attain the work's central message. Of all
Camus's texts, *The Fall* has generated the broadest
diversity of critical readings precisely because of the
apparently uncontrollable multiple meanings that in-
here within its personal *and* allusive potential.

1. Setting and Structure

For readers familiar with the evolution of Camus's
work until 1956, *The Fall* contains a number of sur-
prises. Perhaps the most striking and obvious of these
is the setting of the novel—which is no longer the sun-
infused landscape of North Africa, but the fog-envel-
oped watery horizon of Holland. Drawing in part on his
own remembrances of a short trip to The Hague and
Amsterdam in October 1954 and in part on literary and

cultural artifacts, Camus chose to place the action of his ironical narrative in a location that represented for him the antithesis of the stark geographical and aesthetic sobriety he found dominant in the Mediterranean world. Inevitably, the reader who comes to *The Fall* with a clear memory of *The Rebel* and especially of its lyrical conclusion on the notions of *mesure* (measure, moderation) and *pensée solaire* ("solar" or enlightened thought) will find in the setting of the novel—a tobacco- and gin-filled sailors' bar in the red-light district of Amsterdam—a conscious and studied reversal of the values Camus had sought to define in his philosophical treatise. In the simplest of definitions, we say that irony is a figure of speech whereby one says the opposite of what one means: in the case of *The Fall*, it would seem that the entirety of the text is ironical, in that it "says the opposite" of what Camus had asserted so painstakingly in *The Rebel*. At a first level, therefore, it is possible to see in *The Fall* a belated and textually complex "reading" of *The Rebel* in which Camus, instead of criticizing modern man for not recognizing his limits and for denying his "double nature" as beast and moral being (*HR 381*), creates in the novel's duplicitous protagonist an alter ego who revels in unlimited self-indulgence and in the inauthentic proclamation of his essential superiority. Whereas in the final pages of his philosophical treatise Camus had stated that all equivocal language, every misunderstanding could lead to violence and death, that only "clear language and simple words can save us from this death" (*HR 354*), in his novel he portrays an anti-hero whose language is consistently ambiguous, whose ironical circumlocutions weave a dizzying and obscuring web around the notions of innocence and justice that lie, tantalizing in their near-absence, at the center of the text.

Unlike *The Plague,* in which the voice of Dr. Rieux was that of a chronicler speaking in the name of his fellow-citizens, *The Fall* is constructed as a dialogue in which only one voice is heard, as a dialogue that may be the imaginary projection of one monomaniacal consciousness. The chatty protagonist calls himself Jean-Baptiste Clamence and introduces himself to his silent interlocutor with polite ceremony in an Amsterdam bar exotically named "Mexico-City." As a whole, the narrative is a chronologically complicated, unfolding development on the career and personality of Clamence. The more we read of the novel, the more we know about its protagonist, the more we understand why a materially successful Parisian lawyer who enjoyed the admiration of his colleagues and the adulation of his clients gradually became disillusioned with his profession, lost all self-esteem, and moved to Amsterdam to become "judge-penitent" in a meeting-place for the exiled and disinherited of the modern world. In order to gain a preliminary understanding of *The Fall,* we need to determine who Clamence "is" and how he evolved from his Paris identity to his masked persona at the "Mexico-City."

The narrative is organized into six chapters of moderate length, each of which contributes cumulatively toward the completion of the author's portrait of Clamence. In the first chapter, we meet the protagonist in his bar and discover him talking to an unnamed interlocutor in the second-person formal form. When Clamence, in the first sentence of the text, says: "May

143

I propose my services, sir, without risking importunity?" (*CH 7*), the reader has the impression that he himself is being addressed; indeed, Camus has constructed his text in such a way that the "you" (*vous*) to whom Clamence speaks might be any person who picks up a copy of *The Fall*. This impression is dispelled somewhat later on when the interlocutor begins to assume his own traits of identity and character, when he becomes more particularized as a specific partner in the dialogue, but it is important to the dynamic of the novel that the reader begin by considering himself to be in the position of directly-participating listener.

In the first chapter, we learn that Clamence lives in the Jewish quarter of Amsterdam; that his new "profession" of judge-penitent is "double" (based on duplicity) so as to correspond to the duplicitous nature of humankind (*CH 14*); that he sees in the concentric circles of his adopted city's canals an image of the circles of Hell; and that he has a peculiar fear of bridges (*CH 19*). The entirety of the first chapter takes place in the "Mexico-City": the protagonist bids his listener good night as they leave the bar. The second chapter takes place on the following evening in the same location, at which time Clamence describes in some detail his life as a lawyer in Paris. Throughout his narrative, the protagonist mixes a direct account of his past actions and feelings with general observations on the human condition. After relating instances of his own sense of assurance and self-satisfaction, for example, he concludes: "Such is man, my dear sir, he has two faces: he cannot love another without loving himself" (*CH 38*). The specific illustrations chosen by the narrator as well as his ambitious generalities center on the twin characteristics of egotism and hypocrisy that he finds at the core of human action. Overall, the picture he paints of his past life shows a man in possession of intelligence, wit, charm, and just the right dose of cynicism for the managing of a comfortable existence in a decadent capital city. Yet at one point in his confident story a chink in the armor appears: he remembers an evening when, after a particularly satisfying day, precisely when he had begun to exult in a feeling of power and domination, he suddenly heard an explosion of inexplicable laughter at his back (*CH 42–43*). On that night he never discovered the cause of the laughter, but it continued to haunt him in the following days.

Like the previous two, the third chapter begins in the "Mexico-City," but on this occasion Clamence and his interlocutor take an evening walk through the streets of Amsterdam, so that the comments of the protagonist alternate between the relating of his past existence and occasional isolated remarks on the physical surroundings of the city. In this chapter, Clamence progressively develops the thesis that all human relations are based on the inevitable and interminable alternation between mastery and servitude (*CH 50–57*), then gives an account of his own sexual adventures in which he admits: "In sum, so that I might live happily, it was necessary that the partners I elected not live at all. They had to receive their lives, at isolated moments, from my arbitrary will" (*CH 73*). At this point, when his self-portrait has become decidedly harsh in its unflattering emphasis on unenviable character traits, he returns to the image of the bridge that he had alluded to briefly in the preceding chapters and now explains its origin. In a dramatic three-page passage (*CH 74–76*) Clamence explains how, on one November evening two or three years before he had heard the disconcerting peal of laughter at his back, he was crossing a bridge over the Seine river when he noticed a lone woman leaning over the parapet. Although briefly conscious of her and even sensually attracted to her, Clamence continued on his way until he heard "a noise which, despite the distance, appeared formidable to me in the nocturnal silence, of a body that is cast down on the water" (*CH 75*). Moments later, he heard a repeated cry that grew gradually fainter, but despite these signs of distress and of impending disaster, he did not turn around, but regained the isolated comfort of his Paris apartment. Immediately after the telling of this central, all-determining event, Clamence and his interlocutor conclude their walk upon arriving at the protagonist's Amsterdam home, which the latter describes, significantly, as a "refuge" (*abri*) (*CH 76*). We begin to understand, at the mid-point of *The Fall,* that the complex histrionics of the protagonist are, on one level, a strategy of avoidance: his verbose assertions of a generalized human guilt constitute an attempt to hide from his own guilt, which is specific, concrete, and real.

In chapters four and five, the protagonist and his silent listener go on an excursion to the island of Marken in the Zuyderzee. They observe the picturesque qualities of the island's immaculate and dainty village, then take a boat ride over the calm waters of the shallow dead sea that separates them from the mainland. During this excursion, Clamence explains how his life changed after the original episode on the bridge, how henceforth he began to discover, under every apparently altruistic action he performed, an essential core of egocentric self-aggrandizement. In a striking formula from chapter four, he says: "after long hours of self-study, I uncovered the profound duplicity of the human being. I understood then, from excavating within my memory, that modesty helped me to shine, humility to vanquish, and virtue to oppress" (*CH 90*). As he continued to live with this knowledge of fundamental duplicity, he found that he could no longer perform convincingly in his role as defender of widows and orphans. In a first stage, he determined to disturb the rules on which the law is erected by covering even the most sacrosanct of his poignant pleadings in a "cloak of ridicule" (*CH 96*). Later, unable even to engage in such games, he left the law profession and came to Amsterdam, where he transformed himself from attorney to "judge-penitent." This crucial turn or reversal—from successful and apparently productive member of human society to marginal gadfly—occurred once Clamence decided that absolute innocence is an impossibility, that all people are guilty, that even Jesus Christ falls short of perfection and thereby deserves our "pardon" (*CH 120*). As we reach the end of chapter five, Clamence's remarks become increasingly bitter and devastatingly ironical:

> since we are all judges, we are all guilty toward each other, all Christs in our distinctive ugly ways, crucified one after the other, and always without knowing why ... In solitude, with the help of fatigue, what can you say, one tends to take oneself for a prophet. After all, that's what I am in this place, in this refuge of stone, of fog and of stagnant water, empty

147

prophet for mediocre times, Elijah without a Messiah, feverish and drunk, my back leaning against this moldy doorway, my finger lifted toward the low sky, covering with insults lawless men who cannot tolerate my judgment (*CH 123–124*).

In the sixth and final chapter, Clamence receives his interlocutor at home, in the "refuge" of his apartment. Here, he continues his reflections on the generalized guilt that envelops humankind in the twentieth century but now describes that guilt in unmistakably religious terms, borrowing from Christian imagery for the development of his theories. At the beginning of the chapter, he alludes to an episode in his past that is farthest removed from the narrative present—a period during World War II in which he was interned in a North African prison camp. He explains that his fellow-prisoners, in a desire to create a form of societal order within their group, elected him their "pope." His role was not only that of prisoner-representative vis-à-vis the authorities, but also that of leader and exemplar who incorporated the values of his small society. He assumed his duties playfully at first, but soon began to take himself seriously. One day, he drank the water of a dying comrade, justifying this action to himself as follows: "the others needed me, more than they needed a man about to die in any case, and my duty was to preserve myself for them. Thus, my friend, are born empires and churches under the sun of death" (*CH 135*). With this episode we learn that Clamence's own guilt extends farther into the past than the dramatically presented bridge sequence. At the same time we discover in his own personal adventure an allegory of the political process whereby one individual, in proclaiming his own superiority over others, begins the process of dictatorial domination. The Christian imagery introduced by the ironical use of the word "pope" in a context of misery and duplicity is expanded upon in a further development of chapter six that is fraught with religious symbolism. Clamence asks his listener to open a cupboard that contains a panel from the Van Eyck altar-piece called *The Adoration of the Lamb*. This panel had been stolen in 1934 from the cathedral of Saint-Bavon in Ghent (Belgium), had occupied a conspicuous place on the walls of the "Mexico-City" for a while, then was removed to its current location in Clamence's room. The one panel in the protagonist's possession is generally referred to as "The Just Judges": it depicts famous and morally irreprochable judges on horseback who have come to admire the Mystic Lamb, who stands in the adjoining center panel and who figures the innocence of Jesus Christ. Since the panel of the just judges is no longer in proximity of the Mystic Lamb, Clamence exults in his own private achievement—which consists of having "definitively separated justice from innocence" (*CH 138*). It is this separation that allows him to exercise his duplicitous "profession" of judge-penitent.

At the end of the novel, in what might be an ironical allusion to the concluding pages of *The Stranger* (in which Meursault imagines his own death-scene and the crowds cheering at his demise by guillotine), Clamence fantasizes his arrest at the hands of his interlocutor-turned-policeman, followed by his decapitation in public view:

You would arrest me then, that would be a good start ... I would be decapitated, for example, and I would not be afraid of dying, I would be saved. Above the assembled crowd, you would raise my still fresh head, so that the people could recognize themselves and that once again I could dominate them in exemplary fashion. All would be consummated, I would have achieved, incognito, my career of false prophet who cries in the desert and refuses to leave its refuge (*CH 154–155*).

In his mad imagining of the people recognizing themselves in his decapitated head, Clamence foreshadows the final paragraph of the novel, which is also based on the imagery of mirror-recognition. In a moment of final appropriate irony, the protagonist discovers that his interlocutor is also a Parisian lawyer. What Clamence has been saying throughout his narrative can be considered an echo of what his interlocutor could have said, and might now say if he decides to accept Clamence's invitation to confess his own past guilt. The ending of *The Fall* is circular. Clamence has related a story that can now be repeated by his listener, who, in telling his story, can invite another person to confess, *ad infinitum*. Words engender more words, and guilt is infinite. At the same time, of course, since the interlocutor has never spoken in the text, he may be a figment of Clamence's imagination (the "other" lawyer may be the verbose protagonist's own mirror image)—in which case the supposed dialogue collapses into a ceaseless self-engendering monologue. Doubtless we shall never know which of these stagings—the monological or the dialogical—is the "true" one, since, as Clamence says (truthfully): "It is quite difficult to untangle truth from falsehood in what I tell" (*CH 127*).

2. Some Interpretive Issues

In the foregoing paraphrase, I have emphasized the general structure of the novel—its dramatic progression and overall narrative development. At this point, I would like to return to some of the interpretive problems that I mentioned only in passing in the preceding section. My purpose is not to be exhaustive in my presentation, but rather to raise fundamental issues of the text's meaningfulness that might generate discussion among readers.

a. The Setting and its Connotations

In choosing Amsterdam as the location of *The Fall,* Camus capitalized on historical, artistic and literary connotations that would surround the city in the mind of the cultivated European reader. The novelist emphasizes two periods of Amsterdam's history—its colonial period (the era extending from the seventeenth until the early nineteenth century when Holland administered the Dutch East Indies) and the years of World War II. In the first case, Camus reminds us that the commerce linking Holland to the Indies included trade not just in spices, exotic foodstuffs and aromatic wood, but also in slaves. When Clamence and his interlocutor take their evening walk through the city streets, the former points out two ornamental carved heads on a particularly elegant house: these heads represented "Negro slaves" (*CH 49*) and the house belonged to a man who owed his considerable wealth to the selling of these people. With typical irony, Clamence explains that the only important difference between the colonial period and our modern age is that our rich ancestor had the courage to proclaim directly and emphatically, "My trade is slavery, I sell black flesh" (*Ibid.*), whereas today the successful entrepreneur has more "liberal" views (he will sign manifestoes against man's inhumanity to man), but institutes the equivalent of slavery in his dehumanizing factories.

Just as one is surrounded by evidence of Amsterdam's colonial past, by visual representations of the "sins of the City Fathers," in the same way one is necessarily reminded of the more immediate past—the years of World War II in which the Jewish population of the city (and of the Netherlands as a whole) was subject to persecution, deportation, and ultimate death in Nazi prison camps. At the very beginning of his story, Clamence tells us that he lives in the "Jewish quarter" (*CH 14*), and on several occasions he uses the terms "liquidation" and "washing-clean" (*lessivage*) in alluding to the tenets of Nazi ideology, whereby the "impure" non-Aryan elements of European society were to be "washed out" of the continent in a massive "cleansing" operation. Naturally, the numerous canals of Amsterdam (a city often called "the Venice of the North") played a role in Camus's emphasis on liquid imagery as such, including the unpleasant metaphors of *liquidation* and *lessivage*.

As all tourists know, Amsterdam is also a city of museums. And Holland is associated, in the mind of the knowledgeable European, with the classical Dutch schools of painting that flourished in the seventeenth century. Camus alludes, usually playfully, to this artistic tradition, as when his protagonist reproaches his interlocutor for not seeing, beneath the practical exterior of the city's inhabitants a penchant for decidedly impractical reverie:

> You are like everyone, you take these upstanding citizens for a tribe of syndics and merchants counting their gold crowns along with their chances for eternal life, and whose only lyricism consists of occasionally taking anatomy lessons, covered in their broad hats? You are wrong. They walk near us, that is true, and yet, look where their heads are: in this fog of neon, gin and peppermint that falls from red and green illuminated signs. Holland is a dream, sir, a dream of gold and of smoke (*CH 17*).

In this passage, Camus alludes to paintings by Rembrandt (1606–1669), the great Dutch painter who often took as subjects for his art the scenes of everyday city life, including not only groups of merchants counting their gold in private rooms, but also public anatomy lessons in university amphitheaters. In insisting that the real life of these everyday people is to be found elsewhere—in exotic and undefined reverie—Camus introduces a vision of what one might call the spiritual beauty of Holland: a beauty captured by the French poet Charles Baudelaire (1821–1867) in poems such as "L'Invitation au Voyage." In a number of Baudelaire's most famous works, a specific sensual impression, such as the smell of a woman's hair, produces a complex "analogous" visual representation; touch or smell causes the dreamer to "travel," to voyage beyond the constraints of his present circumstances toward an imaginary world of sensual *and* spiritual harmony. It is quite possible that Camus is thinking of Baudelaire when his protagonist suggests that his listener frequent one of the women of the red light district:

Those women, behind the windows? They supply dreams, inexpensive dreams, voyages to the Indies! These persons perfume themselves with spices. You enter, they pull the curtains and navigation begins. The gods descend on the naked bodies and islands drift by, in a mad vision, covered with palm trees like hair ruffled in the breeze. Try it (*CH 20*).

Of all the reasons Camus had for choosing Amsterdam as a setting—historical, artistic and literary—perhaps the major one was its watery habitat. Water dominates as the single most important symbol in *The Fall,* not only through its own connotative potential, but also in its opposition to other elements and symbols. Thus, when Clamence asserts that the concentric circles of Amsterdam's canals resemble the circles of Hell, he alludes to Dante's *Inferno,* but replaces the imagery of fire used by the Italian poet with his own water imagery (*CH 18*). Later on in the narrative, in describing the "negative landscape" of the Zuyderzee with its blending of grey sky and flat grey sea, the protagonist speaks of a "soft, flaccid hell" (*un enfer mou*) in which "space is without color, life is dead." For him, the watery Dutch landscape represents "universal erasure, nothingness made visible" (*CH 78*). Unlike classical Christian emblems of Hell, which rest on the clear illuminating power of flame, Camus's personal rewriting of our fallen state accentuates the blurring of boundaries, the mental and spiritual confusion of the modern human being, who, abandoned by God and by all transcendence, does not know, in a fundamental sense, where he is. Unlike the Christians, for whom an almighty deity has established the frontiers of good and evil, and unlike the ancient Greeks, who navigated among islands "whose rocky shoreline contrasts clearly with the sea" and where, in the "precise light, all objects serve as points of reference" (*CH 103*), the inhabitants of the modern world make their voyage in liquid imprecision, unaware of all frontiers, unable to find their way against a nebulous horizon.

b. Religion

The Fall is unique among all of Camus's novels in that it makes consistent use of a religious vocabulary. Because of this, some early readers of the narrative hastily assumed that its author had initiated a major change in his philosophical perspective, or even that he had "converted" altogether. As Camus was to declare in several interviews, this was not the case. Nevertheless, the reader of *The Fall* must come to terms with Camus's use of religious themes and imagery as a preliminary step toward understanding the novel as a whole.

In the first place, the name of the protagonist is Jean-Baptiste Clamence—a double allusion to Saint John the Baptist, the New Testament figure who prepares the way for Jesus Christ. Not only is the first name transparently that of the Saint, but the last name, Clamence, plays on the Latin present participle *clamans,* meaning "crying," which is to be found in the legendary expression that describes John's arduous

wanderings and preachings: *vox clamantis in deserto*—
that is, the voice of one crying in the wilderness. From
the very beginning of the novel, Camus ironically
equates the disabused ruminations of his protagonist
with the act of prophecy. But, as we saw in a quoted
passage in the previous section, Clamence calls himself an "empty prophet for mediocre times, [an] Elijah
without a Messiah" (*CH 124*). Elijah was an Old Testament prophet who foretold the coming of a Messiah,
or Savior, long before the arrival of John the Baptist,
whose role was essentially the same as that of Elijah.
What separates Clamence from his illustrious predecessors is his own "emptiness" of character (his moral
vacancy) as well as the fact that, unlike his Biblical
models, his prophecy announces nothing concrete, or
perhaps, nothing real. There is further irony in
Camus's choice of Clamence/*clamans* as a name for his
hero. The epithet of "baptist" was chosen for John for
obvious and literal reasons: his role was to purify, in
the act of baptism by water, those people who awaited
the Messiah (and in the culmination of his preparatory
activity, he baptized Jesus). Clamence, however, is not
only "impure" in a general sense (that is, morally un-
admirable), but the moment at which he could have
demonstrated the courage of a genuine moral choice
occurs when he does *not* jump into the water to save a
drowning unknown woman from death. The plunge
into water that promises purification for the Christian
is the plunge not taken by Clamence.

The essential role of Jean-Baptiste Clamence is to
reverse the values on which Christian morality is constructed. Whereas the actions of St. John and Jesus
exemplified the notion of *agape*—that is, the brotherly

love or charity wherein all humans demonstrate their essential equality and oneness—the actions and the mad fantasies of Clamence center in dreams of power and domination. Thus, when he imagines his own beheading (in an allusion not just to the end of *The Stranger,* but to the end of the life of St. John, whose severed head was presented on a silver platter by Salome to King Herod), it is not as a sacrifice in the name of Christian charity, but rather as a devious method for obtaining the subservient admiration of his "public":

Above the assembled crowd, you would raise my still fresh head, so that the people could recognize themselves and *so that once again I could dominate them in exemplary fashion* (*CH 154–155*).

The very "profession" of Clamence, that of judge-penitent, constitutes a reversal of Christian values. If we imagine a cynical tyrant like Caligula occupying one end of the moral spectrum while Jesus Christ in his infinite charity stands at the other extreme, we should say that Clamence adopts the formal trappings characteristic of the Christian attitude (humility, self-criticism, personal confession) but twists them in the service of his goal, which is that of absolute domination—a moral tyranny at least as potent as the political enslavement practiced by Caligula. The purpose of Clamence's self-debasement is far from brotherly or altruistic in mode: his is a strategy of confessional discourse that aims at the humiliation of his interlocutor. Clamence's genius consists in his discovery that one can humiliate one's opponent at least as effectively by beginning below his level as by reigning above it. Penitence in its strategic Clamencian form is thus merely a step toward attaining judgmental superiority.

The importance of Christian imagery in Camus's novel begins, of course, with the title of the volume. In naming his work *The Fall,* Camus alludes to a primary episode in Genesis in which Adam and Eve, the original human inhabitants of Eden, are driven out of their earthly paradise after disobeying God by eating the fruit of the tree that offered the knowledge of good and evil. The Biblical episode describes man's fall from grace, and his fall into the hardships and constraints of life in the natural and social worlds. Camus plays with the notion of the fall not only when Clamence, in describing his early, self-satisfied Paris days, admits: "free from all duty, removed from judgment and every form of sanction, I reigned, freely, in an Eden-like luminosity" (*CH 31*); but later in the narrative, a woman falls from a bridge (*CH 74–76*); and finally, once he has begun to recognize his own duplicity, Clamence begins to fall, literally and inexplicably, in public places (*CH 83–84*). In Clamence's case, falling relates to the important and pervasive theme of laughter in the novel. To fall in front of one's fellow humans is to lose face, to cease being superior and to become the mere object of someone else's amusement. Camus recognizes that cruelty is never very far from laughter, since both laughter and cruelty derive from the superiority of one person over another. As Clamence progresses toward his final status as judge-penitent, he understands that he can regain his mastery over others by laughing at himself; by becoming a strategic ironist, by forcing his listener(s) to identity with his narrative, he eventually reverses the situation and regains control of his staged dialogue. In his essay on "The Essence of the Comical," Baudelaire asserted that Christ never laughed, that the comical as such, being based on a very non-charitable discrepancy in power between the person who laughs and the object of his merriment, was therefore "Satanic" in mode. It was Satan, disguised as a serpent, who caused the fall of humankind. In his use of mordant irony, in his efforts to undermine innocence and separate it from justice, Clamence aligns himself with his devious, tortuous predecessor.

c. Narration

If Camus's three novels retain the attention of the reading public today, it is not just because of the ideas they express but also because of their subtle and appropriate narrative forms. Camus heightened the dramatic tension of *The Stranger* by constructing it symmetrically around three deaths (that of the protagonist's mother at the beginning, that of the Arab in the middle of the story, and that of Meursault himself at the end). The central placement of the murder scene at the beach calls attention to the centrality of the act within the text; form and content coincide and illuminate each other in this one theatrical moment. For *The Plague,* a work that depicts not the struggle of an individual against his fate but the plight of an entire community, Camus chose the form of a chronicle in which the personality of the narrator is not allowed to intervene. What Dr. Rieux tells of the epidemic and its effects is not in his own name, but in the name of Oran's citizenry. The action of the novel builds slowly and gradually, and has the overall structure of a five-act classical tragedy.

In composing *The Fall,* Camus faced a delicate balancing act. On the one hand, his protagonist being representative of the excesses and unreason of our time, the novelist needed to give him free reign to express himself with appropriate hyperbole; the discourse of Clamence could not appear controlled from the outside lest it lose its power of disorientation and dislocation of the reader's sensibilities. On the other hand, however, for an ironical tale to exercise maximum rhetorical power, it must be tightly constructed and concentrated in its effects. Camus managed to reconcile these two opposite demands through an astute manipulation of the text's formal potential. By structuring *The Fall* as a conversation in which only the "unhinged" protagonist speaks, and by allowing the conversation to seem interminable in its labyrinthine meanderings as it stretches over several days and several landscapes, the author draws his reader into Clamence's web, into the dizzying perverse logic of his duplicitous arguments. At the same time, however, underneath the simple chronological progression of the conversation (from the initial meeting in the "Mexico-City" through the evening walk in the city to the excursion on the Zuyderzee to the final meeting in Clamence's room), Camus has created a subterranean temporal archaeology that the reader gradually excavates as he moves toward the conclusion of the book. It is the subtle and complex layering of temporal levels that gives *The Fall* its density and that allows the narrative to say so much so elliptically.

Although Camus does not intend his novel to be "realistic" in the classical sense (for this reason, very few specific dates are to be found in the text), nevertheless he makes it possible for the reader to reconstruct five separate narrative levels, which I shall designate by number, moving from present to most remote past:

1. Current Conversation: the dialogue between Clamence and his interlocutor that begins in the "Mexico-City" one evening and concludes just a few days later in Clamence's room. We are in post-War Europe, most likely in the late forties or early fifties.

2. Clamence's Recent Past in Amsterdam: in various rapid allusive comments, the protagonist relates his early days in the Dutch city and his assumption of the role of judge-penitent. It is during this period that the Van Eyck painting appears, first on the wall of the "Mexico-City," then in Clamence's apartment.

3. Clamence's Life as Lawyer in Paris: this period includes the early days of self-satisfaction as well as the uncomfortable episodes on the bridges of the city and the fundamental discovery of man's "double nature." Since the protagonist's age is never given, we do not know whether he began his practice of law before or after the war. We can assume, however, that at least a good part of what he describes at this level occurs immediately after 1945.

4. Clamence's Life in Prison Camp: this episode takes place during World War II after 1942 (we know this because the narrator alludes briefly to the Allies' occupation of North Africa via "Operation Torch"). From this temporal layer subsists only the one crucial remembrance of the "pope" adventure, in which Clamence learns about the birth "of empires and churches, under the sun of death" (*CH 135*).

5. The Theft of the Van Eyck Painting: this is an actual historical event that took place in 1934 (the "Just Judges" panel of the altar-piece was indeed stolen and its unknown location was a matter of speculation for years). Clamence is, of course, not the original thief, but he participates in the process whereby the painting remains removed from its rightful place and hidden from public view.

Like *The Stranger, The Fall* is constructed around a central point. Just as it is necessary to grasp the importance of the murder scene in the first novel, in the same way our interpretaton of *The Fall* as an aesthetic unity will depend on the way in which we read the scene on the bridge in which Clamence does not act. In a fundamental sense, the dramatic center of *The Fall* occurs at the deepest remove of level 3, the original bridge scene that splits the protagonist's life into a "before" of unquestioning egocentric pleasure in a kind of "Eden" and an "after" of duplicity in the self-chosen role of judge-penitent. Level 5 remains outside the essential narrative frame and relates to level 2; level 4 adds depth to our understanding of Clamence's human weakness and lends resonance to the pervasive theme of political domination, but it does not have the central causative status of the episode on the bridge.

In a curious way, *The Fall* appears to be a studied re-writing of *The Stranger*. Both texts center on an individual, on a central moment in which he acts in a criminal fashion, and on the problem of his guilt and moral responsibility. In *The Stranger,* the entirety of the novel hinges on the murder scene and on the way in which the reader chooses to judge the protagonist's involuntary, dream-like killing of the Arab. Although

the rhetoric of the novel manipulates us to find ultimate guilt not in the hero but in society, we must examine Meursault carefully before concluding that he
is innocent. In *The Fall,* the central event is not a
violent action, but a passive avoidance of all human
intervention. In the eyes of the law (of society)
Clamence is less guilty than Meursault; after all, the
law does not prescribe that we must jump off bridges
to save people we do not know. Nevertheless, the rhetoric of the text has us believing, from the very beginning, in the guilt of the protagonist; there is no
question that Clamence is not only guilty of a specific
crime of passivity, but that he incorporates and exem-
plifies the moral nullity of our time. Between the publication of *The Stranger* and the appearance of *The
Fall* lies World War II and its immediate aftermath.
Gone is the Romantic pathos with which Camus por-
trayed Meursault as pursued by blind fate and misunderstood by a hypocritical society. As he demonstrated
in *The Plague,* evil is not conveniently located in an
exterior social or political entity, but lies dormant
within us all. *The Fall* moves beyond the sober expository clarity of *The Plague* and manifests the ubiqui-
tous presence of evil within logic and within language
itself. We know we are guilty, but a serpentine trajec-
tory through language can make of our confession the
persuasive proof of another's guilt. The perverse form
of satisfaction, even joy, that derives from our infecting
other humans with our own moral insufficiency is a
characteristic of human behavior few authors have
analyzed with the depth and cunning of Camus. With
The Fall, in an explosion of formal and rhetorical brilliance, Camus wrote his most allusive, most demand-

ing, and most complex work. In his last novel, he diagnosed the ills of the age but offered no solutions, no prescriptions for an improving of the human condition. In *The Fall* Camus gave literary form to the excesses (*démesure*) he had criticized in *The Rebel*. Unlike the serious philosophical treatise, however, the ironical novel remains within the foggy confusion of Northern climes. Ironically, it may be that by sinking into this darkness Camus achieved a higher clarity of perception and judgment than in his nostalgic solar myth of a disappearing Mediterranean unity.

CHAPTER SIX

L'Eté (Summer)
and
L'Exil et le royaume (Exile and the Kingdom)

From the time of the publication of *The Rebel* in 1951 until his death in January 1960, Camus was to be continually preoccupied with one of the central and most controversial political issues in France at that time: namely, the "Algerian question." Since 1830 Algeria had been colonized by the French, and by 1954 the number of native French citizens living in Algeria had reached one million out of a total population of eleven million. The young Albert Camus growing up in Algiers went to French schools and was taught the rudiments of the French language and culture in an "overseas department" administered by a prefect who was appointed from Paris. Because many of the French minority had lived in Algeria for several generations, they did not consider themselves to be foreigners or even settlers in their adopted land, but rather the proprietors and masters of a rich agricultural and developing industrial territory.

As historians and sociologists have taught us in recent years, nineteenth-century colonialism was not always a subtle affair. Typically, the European colonizing nations imposed their own values and cultural norms on the native populations, which enjoyed only a subservient, second-class status within the social hierarchy. In the specific case of Algeria, the unique route to achievement and success for a native of that country passed through the French language, the French schools, and French culture. During the first century of French colonial administration the misery of the Moslem and Berber populaces was evident and real, but no political forum existed for the expression of their grievances. Furthermore, because of the diversity of customs, religious beliefs and forms of social organization to be found among the inhabitants of the territory, it was not until the 1940s that the very notion of a distinct and defined *nation* of Algeria began to emerge among largely secretive and not yet cohesive anti-colonial nationalist factions.

Whereas relative calm characterized the political scene in Algeria during Camus's childhood, the climate changed radically during the 1950s, when the nationalist movements became stronger and more politically effective, and when the French administration grew increasingly repressive in its methods of insuring its own domination. Since the end of World War II and until his death, Camus and his family were to live in France. No longer in close touch with the day-to-day political and social reality in Algeria, Camus had difficulty adjusting his own strong views to the rapid changes that were definitively altering the balance of power in his homeland. Until his death Camus remained convinced that the only just solution to the "Algerian problem" was in compromise and rational cohabitation or "fraternization": that is, Algeria should remain a French territory or department, but should also enjoy a special status in some areas; most importantly, the Moslem majority should have parliamentary representation and full rights protected by the law. On the one hand, therefore, Camus never questioned the legitimacy of a French administrative power structure; on the other hand, however, as he demonstrated unequivocally in his own actions and writings, he believed in the fundamental equality and dignity of all groups residing in his land. Camus's intellectual and cultural interests were not exclusionary: he envisioned an Algeria in which Moslem, Berber, Frenchman and Jew could live together in harmony, each individual respecting the diverse cultural heritage of his fellow citizen.

It is possible to distinguish three stages of Camus's involvement in the "Algerian question" during the 1950s. At first, immediately following the publication of *The Rebel* and his controversy with Sartre, Camus looked to Algeria as a homeland in which to seek inspiration and rediscover the source of his artistic productivity. In December 1952 he went to Algeria alone. Not only did he visit some of his favorite places located not far from Algiers, such as Tipasa, but he also made an extensive trip by automobile through various oasis towns in the Sahara territories. To this trip we owe the important lyrical essay entitled "Retour à Tipasa" ("Return to Tipasa") that was published in the volume *L'Eté* (*Summer*) in 1954, and also the masterful short stories "La Femme adultère" ("The Adulterous Woman") and "Le Renégat" ("The Renegade"), which were included in *L'Exil et le royaume* (*Exile and the Kingdom*) (1957). From what we know of Camus's life, it appears that this short return to his native land constituted welcome if momentary relief from the frustrations of the Parisian limelight. He came back to France convinced that the source of his literary creativity still lay in the sun, the sea, and the ancient stones of Algeria.

From mid-1955 until early 1956 Camus entered a second, much more political stage of involvement with Algerian matters. As of May 1955 he began to contribute articles, on a regular basis, to the newspaper *L'Express* (this periodical was to assume a much larger format the following year, and now resembles *Time* or *Newsweek*). Several of his most passionate articles, later to be collected in the volume *Actuelles III,* urged conciliation among the now increasingly belligerent factions in the Algerian struggle. As a result of his journalistic interventions, which attracted the notice of the Algerian press and political parties, Camus was invited to speak at a large meeting, held in the Arab quarter of Algiers, that had been organized by a group of liberal *pieds noirs* and of moderate Moslems (the French and the Moslems were working together in an attempt to reach a compromise solution and to ward off what seemed to be inevitable bloodshed). This meeting took place on January 22, 1956, and Camus did indeed speak, but the atmosphere inside and outside of the vast hall chosen for the colloquium was tense. While he was speaking, Camus could hear a crowd of French *ultras,* or far-right conservatives, shouting outside the windows and demanding his execution (even before leaving France, Camus had received letters from Algeria containing death-threats). Clearly, Camus's ideas of reconciliation were out-of-season, not only because the conservatives had hardened their position, but because several of the so-called Arab "moderates" at the meeting had already become clandestine members of the Moslem nationalist coalition called the Front de Libération Nationale, or F.L.N. Having left Algeria under protective escort, Camus returned to France discouraged over the prospects of peace and political harmony in his homeland.

In a third and final stage, Camus witnessed from afar the transformation of Algeria into an armed camp. He made a short trip to Algiers in March 1958 in celebration of his recent Nobel Prize, but this visit was nonpolitical. As of May 1958, with the return of Charles de Gaulle to power in the newly constituted Fifth Republic, the fate of Algeria was sealed: after some short-lived initial hesitations and ambiguities, de Gaulle used his considerable prestige to effect the metamorphosis of Algeria from French department to independent nation. Camus died two years before the official proclamation of Algeria's statehood. Of crucial importance to the Camus scholar is the fact that the author's final, unfinished work, is a manuscript entitled *Le Premier Homme* ("The First Man"), a novel set in Algeria that describes, often in transparently autobiographical terms, the sentimental education of a young man whose character develops in harmony with his natural and cultural surroundings. Ironically, it is precisely at the moment of his country's political disintegration that Camus feels compelled to write a novel which, in many ways, can be read as a powerful hymn to Algeria, as a profession of faith in its enduring physical beauty and cultural sustenance. In his final years, it is safe to say, Camus focused increasingly on his relation to his homeland: for him, the "Algerian question" contained not only a political, but most importantly, a personal dimension. For the writer residing in Paris, Algeria remained the origin, the center, the source from which he derived both creative energy and moral fortitude.

I. *L'Eté* (*Summer*)

Published in 1954, *Summer* is a series of circumstantial essays written between 1939 and 1953 each of which centers either on aspects of Algeria (its customs, its natural beauty, its cultural artifacts) or on the artistic process. *Summer* does not contain Camus's best work, and some of the essays merely rehearse the recurrent themes of the author—themes that are developed with more depth and conviction elsewhere. Thus, for example, the chapter entitled "L'Exil d'Hélène" ("Helen's Exile"), first written in 1948, with its remarks on Greek thought, the totalitarian impulses in northern Europe, and the notions of *limite* and *mesure,* is obviously a concentrated first draft of what will become, in 1951, the conclusion of *The Rebel.* Similarly, Camus's somewhat terse, occasionally elliptical comments on the role of the artist and the limitations placed on his freedom by society are expressed with less brilliance in the essay "L'Enigme" ("The Enigma") (1950) than in the short story "Jonas" which appeared seven years later, in *Exile and the Kingdom.* Although the first essay of the collection, "Le Minotaure ou la Halte d'Oran" ("The Minotaur, or Stopping in Oran"), traces a lively portrait of Algeria's second city and of its rivalry with Algiers, its date of original publication—1939—renders it necessarily anachronistic to the informed reader of 1954, who senses that the Algeria of Camus's past may be irrecoverably lost. The modern-day French editors of Camus's works in paperback chose, intelligently, to publish *Summer* and *Nuptials* together in one volume: in a sense, the main value of the former lies in its thematic fidelity to the latter; *Summer* repeats *Nuptials* and remains within the aesthetic contours of its predecessor and model.

For the surrealists, existentialists, and other opponents of Camus in the mid-fifties, *Summer* seemed to provide convenient documentary proof that the author of *The Stranger* and *The Plague* had lost his inspiration, no longer had anything essential to say. It appeared that, since *The Rebel,* Camus was reduced to searching through his files for old or even outdated articles to re-publish, so as to keep his name, if not his talent, alive. From his journals and private correspondence we know that Camus was depressed after the publication of *The Rebel,* and that this depression exerted a strong hold over him, intermittently, until his death. Between 1952 and 1960 only the short novel *The Fall* and the collection of polished stories contained in *Exile and the Kingdom* could be compared to the earlier literary works in originality, depth of reflection, or formal completion. Even uncritical admirers of Camus had to be uncomfortable with some of the essays of *Summer,* which were no more than statements of personal taste and opinion, no more than artistically refined vignettes from what might be called the author's "travel-guide" to Algeria.

The one essay in *Summer* that does not fall into the category of merely occasional literature is "Retour à

Tipasa" ("Return to Tipasa"), which Camus wrote immediately following his December 1952 trip to Algeria. Here, Camus is in full possession of his talents as lyrical essayist; here, we sense the exhiliration of a writer who returns to the source of his art without excessive nostalgia, but with a clear vision of the difficult aesthetic and moral equilibrium on which the unity of his literary endeavor depends.

"Return to Tipasa"

In the opening section of his essay, Camus sounds a cautionary note: "Certainly it is a sign of folly (a folly that is often punished) to come back to the place of one's youth and to wish to relive at age forty what one loved with passion at twenty" (*RT 156*). The author of the inspired early essay "Nuptials at Tipasa" realizes that the mere passage of time may have changed both the place he seeks and himself; what he sees may not correspond to his memories, and, perhaps more poignantly, he may no longer be receptive to the message contained in the Roman ruins, the sea, and the mountain range that compose this site. In a brief digression, the author admits to having returned to Tipasa once before (shortly after the conclusion of World War II), and relates his sadness at observing the twisted barbed wire that then surrounded the ruins. At the time of this first return, "in this muddy Tipasa, memory itself became blurred" (*RT 158*): it seemed that the intervention of the war had severed the link between past and present, had rendered the essence of past experience irrecoverable.

Camus's second return to Tipasa is therefore an act

of persistence, a refusal to admit failure. The essayist now pursuing his literary career in Paris knows that he lacks something, and that that something exists, can be recovered or uncovered at Tipasa. Camus feels that he has devoted too much time in these early post-War years to political journalism, to what he calls "an exclusive attention and service to human misery." This narrow focus on the righting of social wrongs has meant "the renunciation of beauty and of the sensual happiness that accompanies beauty." What the essayist seeks is a balancing of two opposing forces, both of which exert a strong attraction on his sensibility:

> But, after all, nothing true is exclusionary. Beauty in isolation tends toward affectation, and justice alone ends in oppression. The person who serves one to the exclusion of the other serves no one, not even himself, and, finally, twice serves injustice. A day comes when, by dint of inflexibility, one no longer marvels at anything, all is known, and life consists of mere empty repetition. This is the time of exile, of dry existence, of dead souls. To live again one needs grace, forgetfulness of self, or a homeland (*une patrie*) (*RT 159*).

This passage is central not only to the essay "Return to Tipasa," but also to the entirety of the stories contained in *Exile and the Kingdom*. In order to express his ideas clearly, Camus proceeds by a series of polar oppositions. On one side are human misery and social injustice, both of which demand our attention and action; on the other side is the simple beauty of the world, which calls the artist to its service in the acts of contemplation and creation. An exclusive attention to one or the other of these two polarities leads toward dryness, artifice, oppression, and spiritual death; a balancing of the two, on the other hand, guarantees renewal, a return toward life. In the final lines of the passage, Camus opposes the notion of exile (*exil*) to that of homeland (*patrie*). This is the same dichotomy that structures his final sequence of short stories, the only difference being that he substitutes the term *royaume* (kingdom) for *patrie*.

Undoubtedly there is a personal note in these various intellectual oppositions. Especially after the publication of *The Rebel*, Camus saw himself as an outsider, an exile in the Parisian literary milieu. He was tempted to look for his "kingdom" (the source of his inner strength and productivity) in his homeland. Hence the return to Tipasa, which seems to promise a rebirth. Indeed, as the essay progresses, the tone gains in lyrical intensity, and the author affirms, in a rare moment of absolute certainty and triumph: "I found exactly what I had been searching for and which, despite time and the world, was offered to me, and to me alone, in this isolated landscape" (*RT 162*). There comes a moment, in the essayist's encounter with his surroundings, that can only be described as a revelation: the world, in unveiling its meaning to the attentive observer, seems to cease all movement, to present itself as a completely visible and apprehensible picture. At this moment, the accumulated stiffness and dryness, the spiritual "petrification" of the observer, melt away:

It seemed that the morning had become fixed, that the sun had stopped in its course for an incalculable

174

instant. In this light and this silence, years of fury
and of night slowly began to melt ... I also listened
to the tides of happiness rising within me. It seemed
to me that I had returned to harbor, for an instant
at least, and that this instant would never end (*RT*
162–163).

In this passage, which is suffused with the rhetoric
of Romanticism, the properties associated with nature
(temporal flux, the ebb and flow of the tides) become
interiorized by subjective consciousness, whereas the
qualities that had been attached to the unhappy self
(stiffness, fixity) are projected onto the natural surroundings. Time pauses, the sun "stops" in an un-
moveable picture so that the observer can bring within
himself the "tides" that promise enrichment and renewal. The pervasive water imagery of the passage not
only reminds one of certain particularly dramatic
scenes in *The Stranger,* but also foreshadows key
moments in several of the stories from *Exile and the
Kingdom.* In particular, as we shall see, the essayist's
permeability to his surroundings, which translates as
an interiorization of the tides, resembles the openness
of Janine to the "waters of the night" in "La Femme
adultère." In both cases, the central individual of the
essay or story gains strength and inner assurance from
a momentary revelation in which a certain stiffness of
habitual existence gives way to fluidity, to the sources
of joy that lie dormant within human care.

As he concludes his essay, Camus reiterates his desire "to exclude nothing" and compares his literary
activity to the braiding of "white and black threads
into a same rope stretched to the breaking-point" (*RT
165*). The second lesson of Tipasa, the lesson learned

twenty years after the initial visit, is not confined to the merging of the individual with nature or to a meditation on the presence of "the gods" within our physical reality. Rather, it teaches us that human existence is a balancing between extremes in which the stasis of a perfectly achieved equilibrium is, by definition, impossible. The purpose of the artist who possesses a moral conscience will be to weave the threads of misery and of beauty into one rope; but this rope is subject to constant tension. Only by accepting and remaining within such tension can the work of art be faithful to the human condition: this is the conviction that inhabits the final literary texts of Albert Camus.

II. *Exile and the Kingdom*

Published in 1957, the short stories of *Exile and the Kingdom* constitute Camus's last important finished literary work. Although at the time of publication most reviewers and critics greeted the volume with only mild praise, it seems clear today, with hindsight, that the stories incorporate many of the major themes that subtend Camus's *oeuvre* as a totality, and that several of these precise and formally achieved narratives deserve to be ranked among the author's better writings. In the commentary that follows, I shall examine each of the stories in the order of their appearance within the volume, emphasizing both the structural cohesion of the individual tales and the thematic continuities that link them together.

1. "La Femme adultère" ("The Adulterous Woman")

This story is told in the third person, with a very strong focus on the protagonist, a woman we know only by her first name, Janine. The setting is the Sahara territories of Algeria, which Camus visited during his December 1952 return to his homeland. Janine is accompanying her husband, Marcel, on a business trip. Largely due to the financial hardships caused by World War II and its aftermath, Marcel, who owns a dry-goods store in the city, now feels obligated to sell directly to Arab merchants in the country's hinterlands. For the first time, the couple sets out into the interior of Algeria, which is essentially desert—that is, rock and sand interspersed only occasionally by small oasis towns. The narrator describes in close detail the physical and emotional strain of the trip on the two characters, the geographic particularities of the Sahara region, the frustrations of Marcel the salesman, and, most importantly, an inner revelation or "revolution" that takes place within Janine. The most crucial consequence of the trip is that it opens up to Janine the essence of her past life and traces the path of a possible but perhaps unattainable liberation.

During the first section of the story, the narrator concentrates alternately on the uncomfortable and fatiguing bus ride toward the oasis town in which the couple will spend the night and on the inner thoughts of Janine, which center on her past life—her early days as a young girl, then her marriage to Marcel. On both the level of the present (the bus ride) and the past (Janine's remembrances), the dominant themes are those of separation, anxiety, and alienation. Not only are Marcel and Janine virtually the only French people in a bus full of silent and enigmatic Arabs, but when their untrustworthy vehicle momentarily breaks down, they are observed by a group of Berber shepherds—nomads who belong to this inhospitable territory and who understand its harsh laws better than the colonial French or the merchant Arabs. Beginning with the bus scene, and continuing throughout the narrative, Camus underscores the significant cultural differences that separate the French from their Arab and Berber coinhabitants of Algeria. As Marcel and Janine move farther away from the coastline, they move farther from their cultural and linguistic points of reference, into unknown lands and customs. At the same time, within Janine's remembrances we note a similar sense of separation or alienation. She associates her youth with freedom, and finds in marriage the monotony of a rather mechanical routine existence. At this early stage in the story, however, she does not understand as much about herself as the reader can glean from the narrator's commentary. Thus, as she reflects on her recent life during the bus trip, we read:

> She had eventually accepted him [Marcel], although he was a bit short and although she did not like his avid and brief laughter, nor his salient black eyes . . . But she loved his courage for life, which he shared with the French inhabitants of this country . . . Especially, she loved to be loved, and he had submerged her with his assiduities. By making her aware so often that her existence mattered to him, he offered

her a full life [*A lui faire sentir si souvent qu'elle existait pour lui, il la faisait exister réellement*]. No, she was not alone ... (*ER Ibid.*).

On the surface, this passage does not seem to communicate much more than the simple message: despite some of Marcel's physical and character traits, Janine has grown to recognize his love for her, and therefore, to love him. There are three points in these sentences that deserve comment, however. First, the use of the verb "submerge" to describe Marcel's "assiduities" is significant: Janine does not merely enjoy the attentions of her husband, she is, so to speak, *drowning* in them. His feelings for her are so powerful as to overwhelm her own sense of self. Second, the "fullness of life" she thinks she has attained comes uniquely from Marcel; if she lives, it is *for him*, and not for herself. The original French phrase used by Camus—"il la faisait exister réellement"—appears naive in context, and will gain in dramatic irony as the narrative progresses. Third, the expression "No, she was not alone" serves to remind us that marriage has signified, essentially, a haven from solitude for Janine. The questions that remain unanswered at this point in the story are whether a mere avoidance of solitude is sufficient justification for a marriage, and whether such avoidance does not constitute a more fundamental evasion: that of the individual human from him/herself. As a whole, the passage quoted above makes us wonder whether Janine is not living her life for someone else, with no regard for her own feelings and aspirations.

In the second section of the story, when the couple has arrived at the small oasis town and Marcel has begun his business dealings, we find Janine increasingly divided between her profound sense of exile in this exotic and strange environment and her desire for something else—a "something else" at first completely undefined. Initially, it would seem that what she wants is the peacefulness and beauty of what she imagines to lie beyond the town's walls, in an oasis she has not yet seen:

> In truth she was day-dreaming, almost deaf to the noises that rose from the street along with bursts from Marcel's voice, more conscious, on the contrary, of this sound of a rushing river ... which the wind engendered in the palm trees that seemed so close to her in her imagination. Then the wind appeared to increase in intensity, the soft noise of waters became the whistling of waves. She imagined, behind the walls, a sea of palm trees, upright and flexible, billowing in the storm (*ER 19*).

Before Janine can define for herself with any precision what she desires, the object of her pursuit is represented as a noise that evokes water—first the soothing flow of a river, then the tempestuous clamor of the sea. The wind in the palm trees metamorphoses into an ocean storm: an initial peacefulness seems to promise a far more powerful conclusion.

It is not until the end of the day that Janine begins to sense the magnitude of the changes that are taking place within her. After her husband has finished his negotiations with the local Arab merchants, she accompanies him to the terrace of the town's fort, which overlooks the oasis and the vast surrounding desert. It is in this place, far from her homeland, that she looks outward, into the unmeasurable distance, to discover what she lacks:

> There, yet farther south, at that place where the sky and the earth joined in a pure line, there, she sensed suddenly, something awaited her that she had ignored until now and that nevertheless she had always missed. In the advancing afternoon, the light gradually became milder; from crystalline, it became liquid. At the same time, in the heart of a woman whom mere chance had brought here, a knot that the years, habit and boredom had tied slowly began to unravel (*ER 27*).

The change in the quality of the sun's light from hard transparency to fluid haze corresponds to a change within Janine. The "unravelling" of the knot of habit leaves her open to the savage beauty of the environment, and allows her to glimpse, far in the background, the camp of nomad shepherds—men who, like the shadowy figures surrounding the bus earlier in the day, "possessed nothing but served no one, miserable but free masters of a strange kingdom" (*ER Ibid.*). Janine not only marvels at the infinite liberty enjoyed by these wanderers, but concludes that this "kingdom" (*royaume*) they possess within their apparently dispossessed lives also belongs, in a fundamental way, to her. There is, within her, a kingdom—vast and terrifying in its emptiness, but also exhilirating in its possibilities—to which only she has access.

In the concluding paragraphs of the story, after the couple has gone to bed and Marcel begins to sleep, Janine seems to hear a "call" (*appel*) emanating from "the waters of the wind" (*ER 31–32*)—that is, from the rustling noise of the palm trees. She leaves the hotel room and returns, this time alone, to the terrace of the fort. Here, in a final moment of ecstatic revelation, she opens herself to and is possessed by the night:

> After so many years when, fleeing from her own fear, she had run madly and without a goal, finally she stopped. At the same time, it seemed to her that she had found her roots.... Then, with an unbearable sweetness, the water of the night began to fill Janine, submerged the cold, and rose little by little from the center of her being and gushed forth in uninterrupted waves toward her mouth now moaning. An instant later, the entire sky stretched above her, overturned on the cold earth (*ER 34*).

It is only at the conclusion of the narrative that we understand its title. Janine has committed adultery with the night. She has been unfaithful to her husband, not in the literal sense, but figuratively: she has left his embrace to join with the night, a night that has turned from crystalline to liquid, and that has penetrated her to transform her being. Henceforth Janine will know that she, as an individual, must be faithful to the inner kingdom within herself if she wishes to enjoy the hard-won freedom of the nomads. When she returns to the hotel room and Marcel awakens, and when he sees her crying without apparent cause, her response—the final words of the story—contain a deep ambiguity: "It is nothing, my dear, she said, it is nothing" (*ER 35*). On one level, of course, what she says is a "white lie": she simply wishes to avoid questioning by her husband, and does not want to relate the significance of her experience in/with the night. On a deeper level, however, what she says is true. The experience she has had is with the essential "nothingness"—the inner desert, the emptiness within the self—that constitutes the ground of being. She has encountered the nothingness from which, if she takes the necessary risks, she can re-form her life. Camus leaves us with a woman who has seen the foundation of her existence revealed and who has discovered that the mere avoidance of solitude through association with another human being can hide that more meaningful solitude that resides within us and whose signs it is our task to decipher.

2. "Le Renégat, ou un esprit confus" ("The Renegade")

In the literal sense, a renegade is a person who has renounced his religion. In its figurative and more usual meaning, we use the term renegade to describe anyone who has abandoned a cause, a political party, a country, or a set of beliefs. In the second story of *Exile and the Kingdom,* Camus depicts a man confused in mind and spirit who has been a traitor to his Roman Catholic beliefs, and who has converted to a primitive and violent form of idol-worship. The purpose of the story is to trace the inner evolution of the man's thoughts, from his youthful enthusiasm for the life and teachings of Jesus Christ to his later abject and cynical embrace of a religion of hate.

"The Renegade" resembles *The Fall* in two essential ways. First, its exceedingly verbose and ironical protagonist weaves a devious rhetorical web in which he attempts to enmesh his reader. It is impossible to read the narrative without becoming absorbed in its meandering confusion, or "anti-logic." Second, one effect of the story is to invert or reverse the serious theses of *The Rebel,* especially the concluding section on "solar" or enlightened thought and Mediterranean *mesure.* Indeed, "The Renegade" is an even more extreme instance of the rhetoric of excess or *démesure* than *The Fall,* and its use of solar imagery in a distinctly anti-Cartesian context has a profoundly destructive sardonic resonance for the reader of Camus's philosophical treatise. The renegade described in the story is a rebel with the wrong cause, a man who has said no to innocence and yes to a blind and perverted form of "justice."

Until its final sentence, "The Renegade" is a monologue with an exclusive focus on the unnamed protagonist. The narrative advances on two temporal levels: 1. that of the frame sequence, which depicts the protagonist in the narrative present as he hides from his "tormentors"; this sequence begins just before sunrise and ends at sunset of the same day; 2. that of the man's past, from youth until the present. As the story progresses, level 2 becomes increasingly close to level 1, until the two virtually merge in one final simultaneous instant—the death of the renegade.

We learn from the sporadic revelations of the second narrative level that the protagonist grew up in the Massif Central, the sparsely populated mountainous region of the French interior that happens to be the only area of the country in which Protestants outnumber Catholics. (Beginning in the sixteenth century during the bloody Wars of Religion, Protestants sought refuge here from religious intolerance and persecution.) Our protagonist was a fervent Catholic and reveled in his minority status. When he later went to seminary in Algiers, he distinguished himself by his self-deprecation and by his desire to seek the most difficult tasks to perform, the most arduous tests of his faith. He had learned that a savage and idolatrous populace lived in the remote town of Taghâza; without hesitation, he robbed the treasurer's office of the seminary, cast off his habit, and traveled across the Sahara to convert the recalcitrant inhabitants of this remote and inhospitable place. Now the enlightened believer from the Massif Central found himself in another world, in a cultural and linguistic situation to which he had no access, among proud and enigmatic strangers who worshipped a Fetish—a carved image in whose magical power they entrusted their lives and those of their prisoners and slaves.

The entirety of "The Renegade" centers on the problem of mastery or domination. At first, while he is still at seminary, the protagonist dreams of the way in which he will "subjugate these savages, like a mighty sun ... I dreamed of absolute power, a power that drives knees to the ground, that forces the adversary to capitulate, and finally to convert" (*ER 43*). When he arrives at Taghâza, however, it is he who is converted to the religion of the Fetish, it is he whose knees fall to the ground in servitude and adoration of his new masters. Camus's allegory is as violent as its message is clear. The sorcerer who guards the idol cuts out the protagonist's tongue and obtains from him total subservience and compete fidelity to a new "god." This brutality seems to be a literalization of the renegade's own dreams of total domination, an ironical turnabout whereby one form of absolutism is simply replaced by another. Adding to the irony is the fact that the removal of his tongue in no way silences the protagonist, who continues to garble and to ramble in a chaotic jumble of words.

The forced conversion of the once-believing, clear-thinking Roman Catholic into a confused but fanatic idolator involves the destruction of logical distinctions and of all forms of intellectual and spiritual subtlety. When, in the final stages of the story, the renegade describes his refusal of Christianity and his turn toward the power of the Fetish, he asserts:

> He [the Fetish] was my salvation, my only master, whose undeniable attribute was evil; there are no good masters. ... I abandoned myself to him and I approved his malicious order, I adored in him the evil principle of the world ... I renounced the long history that I had been taught. I had been fooled, only the reign of evil was without flaws, I had been fooled, truth is square, heavy, dense, without nuance; the good is a dream, a project continually deferred and pursued with exhausting effort, a limit one can never reach, its reign is impossible. Only evil can attain its limits and reign absolutely, it is evil that one must serve to establish its visible kingdom [*royaume*] (*ER 54*).

In "The Renegade," Camus has accomplished the fictional realization of the nightmarish alternations between mastery and servitude that he had described as "modern nihilism" in *The Rebel*. The temptation of modern man, according to the philosopher-essayist, is to dream of absolutes, of totality, of a truth that does not admit any shades of gray. Evil is preferable to good because of its flawless density, because, in the renegade's words, it "attains its limits." One can see an obvious political application here: totalitarian solutions appeal to those leaders who refuse the compromises necessary to the democratic process, who erect the absolutes of ideology above the constitutive limitations of the human condition. Camus's tale of one man's mad descent into evil is a cautionary one: on such experiences as the renegade's are built "empires and churches, under the sun of death" (*CH 135*).

The two images that predominate in the story are those of the sun and of salt. Rather than signify clarity or measure as it does in *The Rebel,* here the sun symbolizes brute force and the inevitability of a harsh fate. As the sun moves across the sky toward the western horizon, the protagonist's tale nears its end, which is his own death. In an act of fanatic fidelity to his new masters, he has killed the missionary chosen by the Church to replace him; but this very act will have alerted the colonial authorities, who doubtless will decide to crush all resistance to "civilization" and Western religion within Taghâza. Thus the renegade's act of faith toward the Fetish becomes, ironically, one of treason: he has made inevitable the demise of the town and the destruction of the Fetish he serves. He becomes twice renegade. It should be no surprise, then, that the sorcerer, at the very end of the story, comes to silence his unruly servant. In the final sentence, a third-person narrator appears rapidly and discreetly to tell us: "A handful of salt filled the mouth of the talkative slave" (*ER 60*).

From the beginning of the narrative, the protagonist refers to Taghâza as "the city of salt" (*ER 44*). Salt not only covers the dwellings in the town, but it seeps into the water supply. It is everywhere—in the earth, in the wind, in the inhabitants' clothing. During the very early stages of his stay in the town, when he still holds Christian beliefs, the renegade prays to God for rain to wash away the salt: "Rain, my Lord, one great, long, lasting rain, the rain of your heaven!" (*ER 45*). Here, Camus may be referring to the Biblical episode of Sodom and Gomorrah that occurs in Genesis 18 and 19. According to this passage, God destroys these two Cities of the Plain because of their evil ways, but decides to save their one righteous man, Lot, and his family, whom he sends to a safe place called Zoar. God has warned his chosen people not to look back on the destruction he will perform; but Lot's wife disobeys: "The sun had risen over the land as Lot entered Zoar; and then the Lord rained down fire and brimstone from the skies on Sodom and Gomorrah. He overthrew those cities and destroyed the Plain, with everyone living there and everything growing in the ground. But Lot's wife, behind him, looked back, and she turned into a pillar of salt" (*The New English Bible,* Oxford and Cambridge University Presses, 1970, p.19). Camus seems to have replaced the Biblical rain of fire and brimstone with the notion of a purifying liquid rain, but his use of salt symbolism reflects that of the Genesis account rather faithfully. The inhabitants of Taghâza, like Lot's wife, have become "pillars of salt" through their distrust, through their lack of belief in the one God. Like Lot's wife, they have turned in the wrong direction, and they thus risk the wrath of a jealous God.

In the end, of course, it is the renegade who receives

the handful of salt in his throat and is thereby definitively silenced. It may be that Camus was also thinking of the important salt symbolism that Jesus makes
use of in the Sermon on the Mount, and specifically,
the passage from the Beatitudes in which God's son
exhorts his followers to suffer persecution gladly in his
name:

> How blest are you, when you suffer insults and per-
> secution and every kind of calumny for my sake.
> Accept it with gladness and exultation, for you have
> a rich reward in heaven; in the same way they perse-
> cuted the prophets before you. You are the salt to the
> world. And if salt becomes tasteless, how is its
> saltness to be restored? It is now good for nothing
> but to be thrown away and trodden underfoot (Mat-
> thew 5: 11–13. *New English Bible,* p. 7 of New Testa-
> ment).

The protagonist began precisely as a believing
Christian willing to suffer all manner of insults for his
God, as a man seeking to follow the path of the proph-
ets. He fully expected his "rich reward in heaven." But
his own power of faith did not stand up to the test, and
he was ultimately to be "thrown away and trodden
underfoot." Because he lost the foundation of his belief
(the "saltness" of the salt), he perishes, ironically, by
choking in the salt provided by the sorcerer. We say,
in a familiar vein, that someone who promises too
much and does not deliver must "eat his words": in
this case, the man who should have been "salt to the
world" must swallow and perish by the very element
that he lacks.

Of all the stories in the collection, "The Renegade"

remains the most mysterious, the most open, in its allusiveness, to critical speculation. Whatever the reader's final opinions on its various levels of significance, the tale stands as a brilliant stylistic exercise and as a disconcerting elaboration of absolutism and nihilism carried to their limits in a monomaniacal imaginative frenzy.

3. "Les Muets" ("The Silent Men")

In the third story of the collection, Camus moves from the realm of the metaphysical to the concrete, everyday world. He describes a conflict between the workers in a small coopers' shop and their boss, as seen through the eyes of Yvars, a forty-year-old experienced day-laborer. The union to which the workers belong has declared a strike on all coopers' shops in the city (unnamed, but most likely Algiers), and the fifteen employees who take orders from Monsieur Lassalle, the owner of the small business depicted in the story, must necessarily follow suit.

At its most immediate level of significance, "The Silent Men" concerns the post-war problem of technological unemployment. A cooper (*tonnellier* in French) is a person who builds or repairs large casks—in the Algerian context, often those used to contain wine. Before the advent of sophisticated machines capable of accomplishing this task, men would fashion the slats of wood, bend them to the proper curvature, and encircle them with iron bars. The work required skill and craftsmanship, and those who engaged in the job could take pride in the result of their labor. Now the cooper's trade was under attack, and was about to become the victim of economic inevitability.

Since Camus is surveying this problem not as a journalist or sociologist, but as a short-story writer, he humanizes the issue and concentrates his attention on individual characters and their mutual interaction. "The Silent Men" is interesting not simply because it addresses one of the crises of modern-day life, but because it examines the central problem—the breakdown of trust and of communication—that occurs when individuals, feeling threatened, turn into themselves and become mute. The entirety of the story could be described as a series of variations on the theme of silence.

We learn at the beginning of the narrative that Monsieur Lassalle has refused the union's demands. The message to his workers is a simple "take it or leave it." Because the latter have been on forced holiday for some time, they now lack money; they return to the shop out of necessity, but with great resentment toward Lassalle. This resentment expresses itself in a first form of silence: Yvars and his colleagues do not respond to their boss when he calls them into his office in an effort at appeasement. We learn that Lassalle's small business is an inherited one, that he lives well but not ostentatiously, and that in the past he has been kind to his employees. One effect of the strike has been to cancel this more humane past in the eyes of the workers: it is as if these former happier days had not existed.

The fundamental question Camus raises in the early stages of his story is that of human dignity. When a person's livelihood is at risk, when it appears that this person's hard-won skills are now superfluous and that he has no value, his very status as a human being is threatened. Indeed, if a machine replaces him, can he lay claim to the respect and concern he deserves from others? This is the agonizing point Yvars ponders before deciding to greet his boss with silence: "Yvars knew ... what everyone thought ... that they were not simply acting sullen, that their mouths had been closed, it was take it or leave it, and that sometimes anger and impotence hurt so much that one no longer has the strength to cry out. They were men, that is all" (*ER 75*).

Until the silent and fruitless conversation with Lassalle, Yvars and the anguish he shares with his fellow workers have been at the center of the narrative. In a sudden shift, however, the narrator introduces an event that changes the perspective. Lassalle's daughter becomes gravely ill and is taken to hospital, perhaps to die. Although Yvars and his colleagues wish to express sympathy to their boss, they seem incapable of doing so. They return home at the end of the day, once again mute.

In this short and simplest of his stories, Camus has constructed a moral dilemma without simple solution. No doubt the union's intentions were good when it called the strike (after all, the union only wanted to better its members' working conditions), but it is questionable whether Lassalle could have acceded to its demands without going out of business. Lassalle was not right to "close the mouths" of his employees, but how is the reader to judge the comportment of the workers when faced with their boss's personal tragedy?

The union, the boss, and the workers have all missed their mark or failed in some way. They have failed, precisely, to be human. They have resorted to unilateral action, to monologue, and have closed the way to genuine communication.

At the end of the story, when Yvars's wife, Fernande, asks him about his first day back on the job, he opens himself for the first time to speech, but utters a nostalgic phrase that cannot be considered a solution or a path out of his current impasse:

> He told her [his wife] everything, holding her hand, as he did during the first years of their marriage. When he was done, he remained still, turned toward the sea, where dusk was already descending rapidly, from one end of the horizon to the other. "Ah, it's his fault" he said. He wished he could have been young, and that Fernande were still young, so that they could depart, toward the other side of the ocean (*ER 80*).

What Yvars desires here is escape from his predicament. In a sense, but only in a sense, he is correct in ascribing guilt or "fault" to Lassalle. But in dreaming of a flight across the ocean to some imaginary haven and in dreaming of a youthfulness that is forever lost to him and to his wife, he stops short of facing the complexities of the human drama in which he is engaged. Yvars's reactions are understandable, and it would be an exaggeration to assert that Camus is condemning his protagonist. Nevertheless, to flee is not to face an issue. At the end of his story, Camus leaves us with the basic problem of communication unresolved, and with the matter of human dignity in abeyance. Yvars deserved better treatment, but Lassalle deserved consideration for his suffering. In the very irresolution of his narrative's conclusion, Camus is suggesting that no genuine social progress can occur until all humans pass beyond the level of accusation, blame, and the univocal ascribing of guilt to the *other* person. In the end, we understand that *all* the men in the story have been silent, and that Yvars's "telling everything" to his wife has not broken through what might be called the silence of the heart—the stubborn refusal to step outside the circle of one's own suffering to recognize and appreciate that of one's fellow human.

4. "L'Hôte" ("The Guest")

As was the case in "The Adulterous Woman" and in "The Renegade," the fourth story of the collection takes place in a secluded area of Algeria, far from the cities, their order and their laws. The narrative centers on a man named Daru, a schoolmaster from France who teaches the indigenous children of this mountainous region the rudiments of the French language and culture. Although no specific dates are given, it is evident that the story takes place during the early stages of the Algerian conflict, when the native population had begun to organize itself against the repression of colonialist rule. In living far from the coastline and from the centers of French influence, Daru is an isolated representative of a civilization whose norms and values are now subject to scrutiny and criticism.

As the story begins, we see Daru in his small dwelling (a simple building that serves as schoolhouse, as storage-place and as Daru's home) awaiting two unknown visitors who are gradually climbing the steep slope toward him. Before they arrive, and before Daru can grasp the significance of their unannounced stay with him, he meditates on his situation in this inhospitable landscape:

In contrast to this misery, he who lived almost as a monk in this lost school, content with the little he possessed and with this harsh life, had felt himself to be a lord [*un seigneur*], with his whitewashed walls, his narrow couch, his bookshelves of pine, his well, and his weekly supply of water and food. Then, suddenly, snow, without warning, without the interval of rain. Such was the country, cruel for living, even without men, who, however, did not make things better. But Daru had been born here. In any other place, he felt exiled (*ER 85*).

In this passage, Camus emphasizes three points: first, Daru's love of his natural environment despite its harshness; second, his privileged status (in relative terms) as a person who can rely on regular supplies and who enjoys shelter and warmth; and third, his dislike of those men whose actions in some way might interfere with his sense of tranquillity. At this early stage in the narrative, Daru feels that he is the "lord" of a barren but beautiful place. Quite transparently, Camus sets forth the enabling opposition of the collection as a whole in the implicit contrast between exile (*exil*) and kingdom (*royaume*) that structures the passage. Of greatest consequence to the story in its development is the fragility of Daru's "kingdom," which appears more threatened by the destructive potential of human beings than by the cruelty of nature.

Indeed, in the following section of the narrative, we learn that the two men advancing up the slope are Balducci, an old French policeman responsible for civil order in this large but sparsely populated area, and an unnamed Arab, his prisoner. The Arab has killed his own cousin, and must be delivered over to the authorities in a town called Tinguit, some distance from Daru's dwelling-place. Balducci, who has other pressing responsibilities, asks Daru to do him the favor of delivering the Arab on his behalf. Since both Balducci and Daru are members of the French colonial community and both are not only subject to its laws but representatives of its values, the policeman's request has some logic and legitimacy. Daru objects that the guarding of prisoners is not his "job." Balducci exclaims in reply: "What do you mean? In wartime, one does all jobs"—to which Daru says: "Well, I will wait for the declaration of war" (*ER 88*).

At the center of the story is the problem of Daru's moral choice. A man has killed another man and justice must be served. Daru, however, does not want to be part of the process of justice; he is not a member of the police, and furthermore, he rejects the world of hate and violence: "A sudden anger came over Daru against this man, against all men and their sordid evil, their untiring hate, their craving for blood" (*ER 89*). Daru refuses to deliver the prisoner, but Balducci leaves the Arab with him; on the following day, Daru will have to make his definitive decision. It would seem that a choice imposes itself on the protagonist. Either he delivers the Arab, in which case he becomes a part of the process that extends from crime to final judgment; or he refuses, frees the Arab, and becomes *persona non grata* within the French social order. The matter is further complicated by the precise status of the undeclared war that is beginning to take place. Neither Balducci nor Daru knows whether the Arab prisoner is "for" or "against" them—i.e., whether he has joined rebel forces or is unengaged in the conflict (*ER Ibid.*)

Between the time of Balducci's departure and the next morning, Daru spends time with the Arab. Camus takes pains to describe Daru as a good host—as a person who welcomes someone he does not know (and who is purportedly a criminal) into his home with sympathy and warmth. In fact, in his hospitable actions toward the Arab, Daru demonstrates a way of living and of being-with-others that stands in stark contrast to the blood fury that has begun to overtake the country, dividing it into Arab rebels on the one hand, and French agents of repression on the other. As we read this section of the story and as Daru gains our sympathy as a character, we should keep in mind the double meaning of the narrative's title: *l'hôte* in French means either "the guest" or "the host." Clearly, Camus is focusing at least as much on the act of hosting as he is on the status of guest (which, incidentally is not only that of the Arab, a guest in Daru's home, but also that of Daru, a "guest" in Algeria).

Although he thinks he hears footsteps around the schoolhouse during the night, Daru finds no signs of intruders upon awaking. He leads the Arab toward the mountains, and, when they have reached a crossroads, points first toward the east (the location of Tinguit, the French administration and police) then toward the west (the plains inhabited by nomads who would be willing to shelter the Arab). Rather than deliver *or* free his "prisoner," Daru leaves the choice up to the Arab. As he departs toward his home, Daru notices that his solitary guest has begun to descend toward Tinguit, and toward French justice. At the very end of the story, upon returning to the school, Daru finds that the chalkboard on which he had drawn a geography lesson (significantly, the four major rivers of France— one of the first facts a French child learns about his country) now exhibits a foreign writing, a message no doubt left by the unseen intruders of the previous night: "You delivered our brother. You will pay" (*ER 101*). In the final sentence of the tale, we read, concerning Daru: "In this vast country that he had loved so much, he was alone" (*Ibid.*).

Viewed as a whole, the narrative moves from one form of solitude to another. In the beginning, Daru was alone but thought of himself as a lord of his environment. Because of the intervention of men (their jealousies, their hate, their blood lust) he now finds himself alone, but in definitive exile. The rocky expanse he once viewed as his kingdom has now become his prison; he is now vulnerable, subject to the wrath of the Arab's "brothers." On one level, there is great injustice in the message on the chalkboard. Daru, the solicitous host, did not, in fact, deliver the Arab to the authorities. In some ways, he may have treated him in a more "brotherly" fashion than the Arab's own violent family. On a deeper level, however, the reader cannot overlook the fact that Daru refused to make a moral choice. By leaving the choice to the prisoner, Daru did not act; he set himself apart from his fellow humans and presumed to pursue his existence in isola-

tion from them and in isolation from the escalating
political conflict in the country. Daru refused to heed
the message of John Donne's much-quoted line: "No
man is an island." By living as if he were alone and
not engaged in the messy complexities of Algerian reality, he separated himself, despite his good intentions,
from those human beings who most needed his support. The ultimate lesson of this story of high moral
drama is that, in some circumstances, the refusal to
choose is already a choice. Daru may not wish to be
part of a judicial process or part of a social/political
conflict, but his non-action, in the eyes of others, *is*
action. To Balducci he is a traitor and to the "brothers"
of the Arab he is the enemy. The welcoming host turns
out to be merely a guest, now an unwelcome one, in a
land that has interpreted his love of solitude as a failure to grasp the constraints and asperities of human
solidarity.

5. "Jonas ou l'artiste au travail" ("The Artist at Work")

The Old Testament of the Bible tells the story of a
man named Jonah whom God asks to go to Nineveh in
order to denounce the wickedness of its citizens. Wishing to escape his duty to the Lord, Jonah embarks upon
a boat instead, but soon he and the members of the
crew are tossed by a terrible tempest. Realizing that
he is the cause of this life-threatening storm, Jonah
volunteers to be thrown overboard; when he is in the
sea, the tempest suddenly stops. Camus chooses to
place before the beginning of his own story the passage
from the book of Jonah in which the reluctant prophet

says to his companions on ship: "Take me up and cast me forth into the sea ... for I know that for my sake this great tempest is upon you" (Jonah 1: 12). The cautionary tale of Jonah is most famous, of course, for what follows this initial episode: when he finds himself in the sea, Jonah soon is swallowed by a whale, in whose belly he lives for three days and three nights. It is not this part of the story in isolation that interests Camus most, however. Rather, the modern writer concentrates his attention on two aspects of the beginning of the Biblical narrative: 1. Jonah's efforts to flee his duty (which in this case is the prophetic denouncing of a city and its sins); 2. the necessity of his punishment and suffering so that his fellow humans can live in tranquillity.

The protagonist of the fifth story of the collection, a painter who not only achieves success in artistic circles, but also a degree of public notoriety, is called Gilbert Jonas. Camus's tale is about the frustrations of the artist in the modern world, about the demands placed upon him by his family, friends, colleagues, rivals, and business associates. In framing his allegory with the Biblical quotation and in naming his hero Jonas, Camus establishes what might be called a one-to-one correspondence between his own story and that of the Bible. Just as the Old Testament Jonah attempted to flee the Lord, in the same way Jonas attempts to escape his artistic duty in various ways; just as it was necessary for the ancient Jonah to suffer so that his fellows might have peace, in the same way, Camus suggests that the artist must live through a certain kind of punishment and pain so that his public can pursue its everyday life in security and without anguish.

"The Artist at Work" is, for Camus and for *Exile and the Kingdom,* a curious, somewhat anomalous creation. It is the only one of the six stories that takes place in Europe (various signs in the tale point unambiguously to Paris); it is autobiographical in an unusually transparent way; and its style can only be described as a pastiche of Voltaire. "The Artist at Work" is a humorous but also bittersweet rewriting of *Candide,* in which the leitmotiv of the Voltairian hero, "tout est pour le mieux dans le meilleur des mondes" ("all is for the best in the best of worlds") is replaced by Jonas's equally naive belief in his "star" (that is: the infallibility of his success, the inevitability of his secure happiness). Like Voltaire, Camus views his protagonist from a distinctly ironical distance, but this distance and this irony are the more remarkable because Jonas, in a crucial sense, *is* Albert Camus. Whereas Voltaire delighted in crushing Candide with exaggerated misfortune as a means of dismantling the tenets of Leibnizian optimism (for which, of course, he had no philosophical admiration), Camus, in loading his hero with the burdens of our hectic modern-day world, was tracing his own self-portrait and was detailing the confrontation between his own naive optimism and the calamities that beset the thinking person in the twentieth century.

The story of Jonas is quite simple and linear in its development. It begins when Jonas is thirty-five years old and his works have attracted the attention of several influential critics. We follow Jonas's career from this early modest success to the apex of his renown in the public eye, then through the eclipse of his name to final obscurity. As the years pass and his artistic work moves through its phases, he marries, has several children, is surrounded then abandoned by numerous hypocritical admirers and false friends, then retreats into ultimate solitude. Beyond the love of his wife and children, there are two constants in his life: the ever-faithful friendship of a man named Rateau, who visits him almost daily, and the regularity of his artistic production, on which he can count until the final stages of his evolution toward silence.

The exceedingly simple narrative framework of the story allows Camus the freedom to express some of his deep convictions on the mission of the artist in the modern world in an apparently off-hand and humorous way. The surface wit of the comments does not remove the sting of the author's observations, however. What Camus has to say about the phenomenon of artistic discipleship, for example, is both funny and sad: funny for the reader to contemplate from the outside, sad (and aggravating) for the artist, who must endure such stupid and non-disinterested "admiration." In the following passage, one hears Camus's own voice:

> Jonas now had disciples. At first he had been surprised, not understanding what could be learned from someone who himself had everything to discover. The artist, in him, walked in darkness; how could he have taught the true paths? But he understood rather quickly that a disciple was not necessarily someone who aspires to learn something. More often, on the contrary, one became a disciple for the disinterested pleasure of teaching one's master....

The disciples of Jonas explained in detail what he had painted and why. Thus Jonas discovered in his work many hidden intentions that surprised him a bit, and many things that he had not intended (*ER 118*).

In this and other similar passages, Camus makes clear that the essential work of the artist takes place in "darkness" and solitude. Whereas the disciples want Jonas to remain faithful to one coherent set of aesthetic principles, the protagonist knows intuitively that the best art does not proceed dogmatically from neat and codifiable theories. As the false admirers progressively invade his life (and his territory: in a literal and physical sense, soon Jonas has no more space in his apartment in which to paint), the conflicts between the artist's natural inclination toward sociability and the demands of his work grow ever greater: "It was difficult to paint the world and men while simultaneously living with them" (*ER 125*).

As the story moves toward its conclusion, Jonas becomes increasingly incapable of painting. This creative sterility, which resembles Camus's own "writer's block" after *The Rebel*, is coupled with a sentiment that might properly be called existential anguish: that is, the less he is capable of work, the more Jonas reflects on the meaning of his existence. When, at the conclusion of the tale, he isolates himself from friends and family in a small loft he has constructed above the rest of the apartment, when he does not lift his brush but merely listens to "the silence within himself" (*ER 138*), he has attained a state of absolute emptiness in which life seems to have become a desert without points of reference, without significance. Only after he has reached bottom does he finally trace one small word on his canvas—a word that can be deciphered either as *solitaire* (solitary) or *solidaire* (solidary).

With conscious intent, Camus has left the ending of his story open. Just as it is impossible for Rateau to determine whether the central letter of the painted word is a "t" or a "d," in the same way it is impossible for the author to know whether he can choose between the privilege of artistic solitude on the one hand and the duty of solidarity with his fellow humans on the other. It is probable that the choice cannot be made, that the position of the artist is always an uncomfortable one—that his career is necessarily an alternation between solitude and solidarity, in which neither side ever permanently attains dominance. In "The Artist at Work" Camus has returned to the same fundamental problem that he developed in "The Guest," where Daru was forced to choose between his preferred solitary life and an act of solidarity—either toward Balducci or toward the Arab prisoner. The difference between the stories is one of emphasis and tone, but in both cases Camus refuses to grant his protagonists—or himself—the luxury of an easy self-involved isolation beyond the cares and conflicts of the brutal, disorderly world in which we all live.

6. "La Pierre qui pousse" ("The Growing Stone")

In the final story of the collection, Camus makes use of personal remembrances from his visit to Latin America between June and August 1949. Having achieved fame as the author of *The Plague,* Camus was much in demand on the lecture circuit, and had accepted the offer of the French government to go on a goodwill tour of cultural exchange. While in the vicinity of Rio de Janeiro, he had witnessed a *macumba,* a ceremony in which Roman Catholic and animist religious rites come together in an explosive trance-like dance. And later, taking a long excursion from São Paolo, he observed, in the town of Iguape, a procession of which the centerpiece was a statue of Jesus Christ, believed to have been carried there by the waves. Both of these lived experiences are central to the dramatic intensity of "The Growing Stone."

The story begins with a lengthy description of a night voyage within the Brazilian rain forest. Camus emphasizes the immensity of the natural surroundings as compared to the insignificance of the narrative's two main characters who, in ferrying their automobile across a "savage river" in a flimsy raft, seem lost amid "the continent of trees that extended beyond for thousands of kilometers" (*ER 150*). The two men are Monsieur D'Arrast, an engineer who works for a French company implanted in Rio, and Socrates, his chauffeur and native guide. The purpose of the voyage through the forest to Iguape is to build a dam in the small village, in order to prevent periodic flooding that threatens agricultural production and causes disease. D'Arrast, with his technical knowledge, represents the values of advanced twentieth-century civilization. The dignitaries of Iguape greet him as a veritable savior, as an individual who can use advanced engineering knowledge and skill to transform the village and bring it into the modern world. His prestige is so strong and so immediate among the town notables that he is asked to dole out appropriate punishment to the local police chief, who, very much inebriated on D'Arrast's arrival, had treated the distinguished foreigner without due respect. (The ceremonious way in which D'Arrast eventually requests the pardon of the police chief merely confirms the cultural superiority of the engineer in the eyes of the town officials.)

The first major theme to emerge in the story is that of Western civilization and its values—as embodied in D'Arrast and as perceived by the villagers. Yet Camus, from the very beginning, makes it clear that the central issue of "The Growing Stone" concerns individuals rather than abstractions. The tale reaches its conclusion before D'Arrast can build his dam, before the reader can determine whether or not the technical mastery of the Europeans will have a positive or negative impact on the villagers—before the question of civilization and values can be posed in an intellectually coherent or systematic way. What the story describes is an inner evolution or even "revolution" within D'Arrast that in some ways resembles the profound encounter of Janine with "the night" in "The Adulterous Woman." In other words, Camus is interested in the representative of "civilization" not for what he may or may not bring to the indigenous population in the way of increased productivity or comfort, but for what he may or may not learn from his confrontation with forces that exceed his rational control.

The primary event of the story is the procession of the statue of Jesus. Socrates explains to D'Arrast that one day the statue arrived in the village, having followed the course of the river from the ocean. Fishermen found it, washed it, and placed it in a grotto, where a stone in its proximity began to grow. Thus what the villagers celebrate through their procession is the miracle of the growing stone. From the moment the engineer first enters the grotto, we understand that his own fate will be bound to the stone in some way:

> Around him the pilgrims waited, without looking at him, impassive under the water that fell from the trees in a fine veil. He also was waiting, in front of this grotto, under the same watery mist, but for what he did not know. He had never stopped waiting, in truth, throughout the month he had been in this country. He waited, in the red heat of humid days, under the distant stars, despite his duties, the dams to be built, the roads to open up, as if the work he had come to accomplish here were merely a pretext, the occasion for a surprise or for an encounter that he could not even imagine, but which had waited for him, patiently, at the ends of the world (*ER 161–162*).

At the conclusion of the story D'Arrast will have this unimaginable encounter; like "the adulterous woman," he will discover a central core of emotion within himself that had been lost or covered over by years of routine activity. But unlike Janine, whose revelatory experience took place in solitude, D'Arrast will change as a result of the people around him—and these people, significantly, are not European. Not only is it worthy of note that D'Arrast's companion is called Socrates (the simple Brazilian chauffeur who speaks broken French possesses, in his own way, a philosophical wisdom—that is, a knowledge of life), but it is especially important to the coherence of the story that

D'Arrast form a strong friendship with another simple native man, a ship's cook who has made a vow to Jesus Christ. Indeed, when he first meets D'Arrast, the cook explains that one night a violent storm overtook his vessel, and that he promised Jesus, if he survived, to carry a very heavy stone (weighing some 50 kilograms, or 110 pounds) during the procession at Iguape. Having been spared, the cook now must make good on his difficult promise. Of greatest significance to the story is the fact that the cook, who does not know D'Arrast and who has no special reason to trust this exotic European, has *entrusted* the latter not only with the knowledge of his sacred vow, but with a certain responsibility: the cook asks D'Arrast to accompany him to the *macumba* on the night preceding the procession and to make certain that he (the cook) does not dance, drink, or smoke excessively. The crux of the story is the testing of D'Arrast: how will he react to the cook's request that night, and what will be the consequence of his reaction when the procession takes place on the next day?

Like "The Guest" and "The Artist at Work," "The Growing Stone" stages the problem of human solidarity. The question is whether D'Arrast can move beyond his own personal concerns and bridge the cultural differences that separate him from the cook: if not, he will have difficulty helping his new acquaintance. In his elaborate and evocative description of the *macumba,* Camus makes it clear that D'Arrast is an outsider in a ritual that owes much of its power to nonrational, magical beliefs. As the dance progresses to its trance-like paroxysm, the cook approaches D'Arrast and, in the name of the assembled company, asks him to leave. The engineer counters: "And your promise?" Without responding, the cook pushes the door. "They remained thus for a second, and D'Arrast yielded, shrugging his shoulders. He departed" (*ER 175*). The shrugging of the shoulders translates D'Arrast's lack of solidarity with the cook. He does not understand the ceremony he has just witnessed, he does not comprehend the "absurd promise" (*ER 165*) the cook has made; rather than insist that the cook leave the dance, D'Arrast departs, establishing a distance between his cares, his mode of living, and the spontaneous emotional frenzy from which he feels excluded:

It seemed to him [D'Arrast] that he would have liked to vomit this entire country, the sadness of its vast spaces, the glaucous light of its forests, and the nocturnal splashing of its great empty rivers. This land was too vast, the blood and the seasons mingled in it, time bogged down in it. Here one lived at soil level and, to integrate onself, one had to lie down and sleep, for years, on the muddy or dry earth. Over there, in Europe, were shame and anger. Here, exile [*l'exil*] or solitude, in the midst of these languishing and excited madmen, who danced to die (*ER 175–176*).

As the night ends, D'Arrast finds himself completely isolated. In Europe are only "shame and anger," and here he sees in the native population nothing more than a "mad" dancing toward a meaningless death. Yet on the next day, when he witnesses the cook stumbling under his impossibly heavy burden, fatigued from the excesses and exertions of the night, D'Arrast intervenes. When the cook falls in exhaustion, D'Arrast picks up the stone, proceeds first in the direction of the church (where the cook had intended to deposit the object of his vow), but then, to the consternation of all witnesses, moves in the opposite direction, toward the river, toward the poorest section of the town. There, in the cook's own hut, where the previous evening's *macumba* had taken place, D'Arrast places the stone. When the cook and his friends arrive at the hut to discover what D'Arrast has done, one of the group, in the final words of the story, says: "Sit down with us."

In the end, D'Arrast has become a member of the community for which he will build his dam. No longer the outsider who is expulsed from the ceremony that unites a people, he has been included in the circle of friendship and trust without which there can be no social cohesiveness. D'Arrast has acted, in part, for himself (in an earlier passage he had admitted to the cook that once someone was caused to die through his fault—*ER 166*—so that his carrying of the stone could be interpreted as his own penance); but it is significant that his assuming of the cook's burden has as its first and principal effect the accomplishment of the cook's vow. In taking up the stone, D'Arrast has acted for someone else; it is this altruism that allows for a renewal of his life.

As was the case in "The Renegade" and "The Artist at Work," "The Growing Stone" contains unmistakable religious symbolism, especially from the New Testament of the Bible. The story concerns a procession that centers on the figure of Jesus Christ. In the early parts of the narrative, the impression of the reader (like that of D'Arrast) might be that the drifting of the

statue on the waves, the adulation of the indigenous
population in the grotto, and the vow made by the
cook, are all indications of superstition rather than
religion in the deep sense. Nevertheless, as the story
progresses, we see that the characters, despite their
limitations, begin to act in a way that mirrors the
essential lesson taught by Jesus—namely, that of
Christian charity. In carrying the stone, the cook necessarily calls forth the image of Jesus bent under the
weight of his cross; and D'Arrast, in helping him with
his burden, imitates the action of Simon of Cyrene,
who is said to have carried the cross of Jesus toward
Golgotha (Matthew 27: 32). According to Biblical
teachings, the most a human being can accomplish is
to bear someone else's burden: to turn away from oneself toward another and his sufferings is the essence
of Christian charity, and also the message of "The
Growing Stone."

In the final narrative of *Exile and the Kingdom*,
Camus has brought together the major themes of the
entire collection: solitude, exile, social injustice, cultural difference, on the one hand; solidarity, community, social equality, and the sharing of cultural
values, on the other. In "The Growing Stone" Camus
has found a delicate balance between the concrete social and cultural issues that inform every aspect of our
daily lives and the metaphysical questions that occupy
the human spirit. His final story concerns Europe and
South America, civilization and its relation to the
Third World; but it also concerns the power of promises, of faith, and of human will extending beyond itself. The preponderance of religious imagery in *Exile
and the Kingdom* in no way indicates that Camus has

"converted" to a specific set of beliefs; rather, it shows that the author of *The Stranger* no longer confines his imaginary universe to mere material cause and effect or to an ancient Greek notion of fate. In his last complete literary work, Camus describes his characters as caught between our immanent reality and a certain mysterious appeal or call (in French: *appel*) that comes to them from a region beyond everydayness, and that resonates within that inner space each of us possesses—a space that can remain as dry as the desert until we heed the call.

CONCLUSION

When he died in January 1960 at age forty-six, Camus
had achieved fame as a writer and as a public figure.
Throughout his career, he had attempted to maintain
a difficult balance between the demands of his art on
the one hand and his social responsibility toward his
fellow humans on the other. Until the end, Camus refused to isolate himself from the important historical
and political events of his time; but as his literary
reputation grew, so did the demands on his commitment to an increasing variety of humanitarian issues.
The Nobel Prize of 1957 crowned a very real achievement (despite the jealous protests of his detractors),
yet at the same time thrust Camus into the limelight
precisely at the moment at which he needed silence
and meditation for a reinvigoration of his creative
power.

Our examination of the chronological evolution of
Camus's essential literary and philosophical texts reveals a strong thematic unity, a progressive mastery
of style, and a deepening awareness of the moral problems that define human existence in the twentieth century. From *The Wrong Side and the Right Side* to *Exile
and the Kingdom,* Camus's thought traverses distinct,
recognizable phases, but it remains true to a central
core of insight that does not change markedly. Indeed,
in a curious way, *Exile and the Kingdom* is a repetition
or re-writing of Camus's first series of essays, in which
the terms *envers* (the "wrong" or "other" side of
things) and *endroit* (the "right" or obvious and visible
side) are merely replaced by another system of polar

oppositions: *solitaire* (solitary) versus *solidaire* (solidary), or *exil* (exile) versus *royaume* (kingdom). Throughout his twenty-year career, Camus describes the painful position of the artist, who is caught between two opposite and perhaps irreconcilable demands. The play of light on window curtains that Camus presents as an example of the "wrong" or "other" side of the world in his earliest work is a first, simple emblem of the domain of beautiful appearances that haunts all true art but that is threatened by the "right" side, the rule of everydayness from which it is difficult for the artist to extricate himself.

Nowhere is the dramatic nature of the opposition between the "wrong" side and the "right," solitude and solidarity more manifest than in Camus's relation to his homeland, Algeria. Although he had elaborated a carefully conceived compromise position on the matter of political rule in Algeria, Camus was, in a sense, no longer an "Algerian." That is, his career was in Paris; he was not in touch with the concrete issues of the moment across the Mediterranean. Viewed in retrospect, Camus's position is all too easily condemned as unrealistic, and his attempts to maintain solidarity with his country seem feeble. At the same time, however, his final works, both finished and unfinished, recreate an Algeria of the imagination that remains poetically evocative to modern-day readers, for whom the political realities of the 1950s are either a vague memory or merely unknown remnants of an historical past. Unable to forge links of solidarity with his homeland at the end of his life, unable to keep physically close to the place (*l'endroit*) of his birth, he transformed this exile into a realm of literary coherence,

214

into a spare and austere *royaume* to which all readers have access.

The works of Camus are the product of an individual who lived in a turbulent period and who could not disengage himself from the contradictions of the historical moment. They bear witness to an age while revealing the talents of one of our important twentieth-century writers. Because of the circular route by which the fictions of the author unerringly repeat themselves, however, and because of the tight, almost extreme coherence of his themes and images, it is legitimate to wonder whether the imaginary universe of Albert Camus emanates from genius or only from a limited and prudent form of literary organization. This is a question for which there is no easy answer, and which exceeds the scope of the present analysis. Perhaps one way to respond briefly, in a final observation, is to say the following: as long as we read works of literature for their artistic perfection *and* for the moral ideas they express, as long as we consider the words of the writer to represent, with care and simplicity, the essential relation of the human being to his world, then Camus's works will remain very much alive at the end of this century.

BIBLIOGRAPHY

Works by Albert Camus

L'Envers et l'endroit. Paris: Gallimard-Folio (Collection "Essais"), 1986. Originally published 1937. [*The Wrong Side and the Right Side. Lyrical and Critical Essays.* Ed. Philip Thody. Transl. Conroy Kennedy. New York: Knopf, 1969. 5–61.]

Noces, suivi de *L'Eté.* Paris: Gallimard-Folio, 1986. *Noces* originally published 1938. *L'Eté* originally published 1954. [*Nuptials* and *Summer. Lyrical and Critical Essays.* 63–105; 107–181.]

L'Etranger. Paris: Gallimard-Folio, 1980. Originally published 1942. [*The Stranger.* Transl. Stuart Gilbert. New York: Knopf, 1946.]

Le Mythe de Sisyphe. Paris: Gallimard-Folio (Collection "Essais"), 1986. Originally published 1943. [Included in *The Myth of Sisyphus and Other Essays.* Transl. Justin O'Brien. New York: Knopf, 1955.]

Caligula, suivi de *Le Malentendu.* Paris: Gallimard-Folio, 1986. *Caligula* originally published 1944. *Le Malentendu* originally published 1944. [Included in *Caligula and Three Other Plays.* Transl. Stuart Gilbert. New York: Knopf, 1958.]

Lettres à un ami allemand. Paris: Gallimard, 1945. ["Letters to a German Friend." *Resistance, Rebellion, and Death.* Transl. Justin O'Brien. New York: Knopf, 1961.]

La Peste. Paris: Gallimard-Folio, 1974. Originally published 1947. [*The Plague.* Transl. Stuart Gilbert. New York: Knopf, 1948.]

Les Justes. Paris: Gallimard-Folio, 1986. Originally published 1950. [Included in *Caligula and Three Other Plays.* Transl. Stuart Gilbert. New York: Knopf, 1958.]

Actuelles: Ecrits politiques. Paris: Gallimard-Idées, 1977. Originally published 1950. [Partially included in *Resistance, Rebellion, and Death*. Transl. Justin O'Brien. New York: Knopf, 1961.]

L'Homme révolté. Paris: Gallimard-Folio (Collection "Essais"), 1987. Originally published 1951. [*The Rebel*. Transl. Anthony Bower. New York: Knopf, 1967.]

Actuelles II. Paris: Gallimard, 1953. [Partially included in *Resistance, Rebellion, and Death*. Transl. Justin O'Brien. New York: Knopf, 1961.]

La Chute. Paris: Gallimard-Folio, 1975. Originally published 1956. [*The Fall*. Transl. Justin O'Brien. New York: Knopf, 1957.]

L'Exil et le royaume. Paris: Gallimard-Folio, 1974. Originally published 1957. [*Exile and the Kingdom*. Transl. Justin O'Brien. New York: Knopf, 1958.]

Actuelles III: Chroniques algériennes. Paris: Gallimard, 1958. [Partially included in *Resistance, Rebellion, and Death*. Transl. Justin O'Brien. New York: Knopf, 1961.]

Discours de Suède. Paris: Gallimard, 1958. (Nobel Prize Speeches of December 10 and 14, 1957.) [December Speech translated as *Speech of Acceptance upon the Award of the Nobel Prize for Literature*. Transl. Justin O'Brien. New York: Knopf, 1958.]

Carnets: mai 1935–février 1942. Paris: Gallimard, 1962. [*Notebooks 1935–1942*. Transl. Philip Thody. New York: Knopf, 1963.]

Théâtre, récits, nouvelles. Preface Jean Grenier. Ed. Roger Quilliot. Paris: Gallimard-Pléiade, 1962.

Carnets: janvier 1942–mars 1951. Paris: Gallimard, 1964. [*Notebooks 1942–1951*. Transl. Philip Thody. New York: Knopf, 1965.]

Essais. Intro. Roger Quilliot. Ed. Roger Quilliot and Louis Faucon. Paris: Gallimard-Pléiade, 1965.

La Mort heureuse. Paris: Gallimard-Pléiade, 1971. [*A Happy Death*. Transl. Richard Howard. New York: Knopf, 1972.]

Journaux de voyage. Ed. Roger Quilliot. Paris: Gallimard, 1978. [*American Journals.* Transl. Hugh Levick. New York: Paragon House, 1987.]

Critical Works

Bibliographies

Fitch, Brian T. *Essai de bibliographie des études en langue française consacrées à Albert Camus (1937–1962).* Paris: Minard, 1964.

Hoy, Peter C. *Camus in English: An Annotated Bibliography of Albert Camus's Contributions to English and American Periodicals and Newspapers.* Second Edition. Paris: Lettres Modernes, 1971.

Roeming, Robert F. *Camus: A Bibliography.* Madison: University of Wisconsin Press, 1968.

Books

Braun, Lev. *Albert Camus: Moralist of the Absurd.* Cranbury, N.J.: Associated University Presses, 1974. A study of Camus's major works in their chronological order, with emphasis on historical context and philosophical issues. A view of Camus as moralist and humanist.

Brée, Germaine. *Camus.* New Brunswick, N.J.: Rutgers UP, 1959. The best overview of Camus's literary works in English. A concise and elegantly written synthesis published one year before Camus's death and containing pertinent analyses of all his major works.

————. *Camus and Sartre, Crisis and Commitment.* New York: Delta, 1972. An excellent comparison of the essential works of Camus and Sartre, with emphasis on the individual style of each author. Indispensable for readers with an interest in the literary manifestations of French exis-

tentialism and in Camus's position vis-à-vis this movement.

Castex, Pierre-Georges. *Albert Camus et 'L'Etranger.'* Paris:
Corti, 1965. Useful though somewhat dated traditional account of *The Stranger* that includes references to Camus's
Carnets (*Notebooks*) and commentary on the author's stylistic techniques.

Coombs. Ilona. *Camus, Homme de Théâtre*. Paris: Nizet,
1968. A useful account not only of Camus's own plays and
adaptations, but also of Camus as actor and director.

Costes, Alain. *Albert Camus et la parole manquante: Etude
psychanalytique*. Paris: Payot, 1973. Interesting, well documented, but sometimes reductive psychoanalytical study
of Camus's work.

Cruickshank, John. *Albert Camus and the Literature of Revolt*. London: Oxford UP, 1959. Excellent seminal study of
Camus's major works with special emphasis on the theme
of revolt—not only in its philosophical conception (*The Rebel*) but also in its relevance and applicability to the novels
and theater.

Fitch, Brian T. *The Narcissistic Text: A Reading of Camus's
Fiction*. Toronto: The University of Toronto Press, 1982.
An important, subtle application of modern literary theory
to Camus's works written by a leading Camus scholar.

Freeman, E. *The Theatre of Albert Camus: A Critical Study*.
London: Methuen, 1971. The best overview to date of the
entirety of Camus's theatrical production.

Gassin, Jean. *L'Univers symbolique d'Albert Camus: Essai
d'interprétation psychanalytique*. Paris: Minard, 1981. A
useful detailed interpretation of major symbols in Camus's
fictions from a psychoanalytical point of view. Occasionally pedestrian in style and tone.

Grenier, Jean. *Albert Camus, Soleil et Ombre: Une biogra-
phie intellectuelle*. Paris: Gallimard, 1987. A readable and
concise intellectual biography of Camus that sheds more
light on the author's life than on his works. Grenier

worked with Camus as a journalist in Paris and has interesting (and presumably accurate) anecdotes to tell.

Lottman, Herbert R. *Albert Camus: A Biography*. Garden
City, N.J.: Doubleday, 1979. By far the most detailed account of Camus's life to date. Required reading for advanced readers and students wishing to pursue their own
study of Camus.

McCarthy, Patrick. *Camus*. New York: Random House, 1982.
Overall, a helpful study of Camus's career and works, but
weaker on the works than on the career. Not at the same
level as Lottman's biography.

Parker, Emmett. *Albert Camus: The Artist in the Arena*.
Madison: The University of Wisconsin Press, 1965. An account of Camus's attempts to balance his artistic objectives
with his political and journalistic commitments. Well
documented and argued with clarity.

Quilliot, Roger. *La Mer et les prisons: Essai sur Albert
Camus*. Paris: Gallimard, 1956. An important early assessment of Camus's career and artistic objectives. By the
Pléiade editor of Camus's works, one of the preeminent
specialists in the field.

Showalter, English. *Exiles and Strangers: A Reading of
Camus's 'Exile and the Kingdom.'* Columbus: Ohio State
UP, 1984. The best interpretation to date of the aesthetic
values of Camus's last completed literary work and of its
place within the totality of the author's *oeuvre*.

Thody, Philip. *Albert Camus: A Study of His Work*. New
York: Grove Press, 1957. A concise study of Camus's works
inclusive of *The Fall* containing good common-sense commentary.

Collected Essays

Camus: A Collection of Critical Essays. Ed. Germaine Brée.
Englewood Cliffs, N.J.: Prentice-Hall, 1962. An excellent

assortment of essays representing a wide variety of critical methodologies. Published two years after Camus's death, this volume contains some of the best literary criticism we possess on the author's works.

Camus 1970: Colloque organisé sous les auspices du Département des Langues et Littératures Romanes de l'Université de Floride (Gainesville), les 29–30 janvier 1970. Ed. Raymond Gay-Crosier. CELEF: Sherbrooke, Québec, 1970. Includes transcriptions of lectures and discussion of an important colloquium on Camus to commemorate the tenth anniversary of his death. One part of the discussion deals with the transformation in the reception of Camus's works in the preceding decade.

Albert Camus's Literary Milieu: Arid Lands. Proceedings of the Comparative Literature Symposium, Vol. VIII. Ed. Wolodymyr T. Zyla and Wendell M. Aycock. Lubbock, Texas: The Texas Tech Press, 1976. Collected articles on the importance of the North African geographical context for Camus's writings. Includes articles by Anna Balakian and Brian T. Fitch.

Albert Camus 1980: Second International Conference. February 21–23, 1980. The University of Florida- Gainesville. Ed. Raymond Gay-Crosier. Gainesville: The University Presses of Florida, 1980. Ten years after its first conference, the University of Florida hosts a second colloquium in which many of the world's prominent Camus specialists participate. A superior collection of essays representing the major currents in Camus criticism.

Critical Essays on Albert Camus. Ed. Bettina L. Knapp. Boston, Mass.: G.K. Hall, 1988. A balanced selection of recent short essays on Camus, but less distinguished and possessing less methodological variety than the *Albert Camus 1980* collection.

Albert Camus: Modern Critical Views. Ed. and Intro. Harold Bloom. New York and Philadelphia: Chelsea House, 1988. A collection that includes several of the most innovative articles written on Camus during the past twenty years. Among others, articles by René Girard on *The Stranger*, Paul de Man on Camus's *Carnets* (*Notebooks*), and Jacques Guicharnaud on Camus's theater.

INDEX

223